INSTITUTE OF LEADERSHIP & MANAGEMENT **ilm**

SUPERSERIES

Making Communication Work

FOURTH EDITION

Published for the
Institute of Leadership & Management by **Pergamon *Flexible* Learning**

OXFORD AMSTERDAM BOSTON LONDON NEW YORK PARIS
SAN DIEGO SAN FRANCISCO SINGAPORE SYDNEY TOKYO

Pergamon Flexible Learning
An imprint of Elsevier
Linacre House, Jordan Hill, Oxford OX2 8DP
30 Corporate Drive, Burlington, MA 01803

First published 1986
Second edition 1991
Third edition 1997
Fourth edition 2003
Reprinted 2006

British Library Cataloguing in Publication Data
A catalogue record for this book is available from the British Library

Library of Congress Cataloguing in Publication Data
A catalogue record for this book is available from the Library of Congress

ISBN 0 7506 5875 4

For information on Pergamon Flexible Learning
visit our website at www.bh.com/pergamonfl

Institute of Leadership & Management
Registered office
1 Giltspur Street
London
EC1A 9DD
Telephone 020 7294 3053
www.i-l-m.com
ILM is a subsidiary of the City & Guilds Group

Working together to grow
libraries in developing countries

www.elsevier.com | www.bookaid.org | www.sabre.org

ELSEVIER   BOOK AID
            International   Sabre Foundation

Editor: Clare Donnelly
Based on original material by Colin Everson
Editorial management: Genesys, www.genesys-consultants.com
Composition by Genesis Typesetting, Rochester, Kent
Printed and bound in Great Britain by MPG Books Bodmin

INSTITUTE OF LEADERSHIP & MANAGEMENT

SUPERSERIES

Making Communication Work

....

has satisfactorily completed this workbook

Name of signatory   ....

Position   ....

Signature   ....

Date   ....

Official stamp

Fourth Edition

INSTITUTE OF LEADERSHIP & MANAGEMENT
SUPERSERIES
FOURTH EDITION

To order – phone us direct for prices and availability details
(please quote ISBNs when ordering) on 01865 888190

Contents

Contents

Workbook introduction

1 ILM Super Series study links

This workbook addresses the issues of *Making Communication Work*. Should you wish to extend your study to other Super Series workbooks covering related or different subject areas, you will find a comprehensive list at the back of this book.

2 Links to ILM Qualifications

This workbook relates to the following learning outcomes in segments from the ILM Level 3 Introductory Certificate in First Line Management and the Level 3 Certificate in First Line Management.

C9.1   Communication process
    1   Understand the concept of the communication cycle
    2   Recognize and overcome barriers to communication
    3   Apply basic theories to ensure effective communication in the workplace

C9.2   Communications media
    1   Select and use the most appropriate and effective method/ channel of communication for a specific situation or purpose
    2   Use non-verbal behaviour as appropriate to specific situations
    3   Check that communication has been properly received and understood

C9.3   Non-verbal communication
  1   Identify range of non-verbal and behavioural factors which affect people
  2   Assess impact of different behaviours in the workplace
  3   Assess impact of appearance and mannerisms in the workplace
  4   Interpret non-verbal signals from others

3 Links to S/NVQs in Management

This workbook relates to the following elements of the Management Standards which are used in S/NVQs in Management, as well as a range of other S/NVQs.

D1.2   Inform and advise others.

It will also help you to develop the following Personal Competences:

■   communicating;
■   influencing others.

The workbook also develops the communication skills that are needed by most other S/NVQ elements.

4 Workbook objectives

You may work in the public or private sector, a charity, the armed forces or a small to medium size enterprise (SME). What is certain, wherever you work, is that your organization will need to communicate information to a wide range of individuals internally, and with other organizations.

I could argue that **all** management is about communication. Management is chiefly the art of getting things done through others. So you can't manage unless you can **communicate** your objectives to the people through whom you intend to achieve them.

Being an effective communicator is an essential aspect of leading and motivating teams in all walks of life, at all levels and in all situations. If you can't communicate, you will be unable to get things done through the team and will end up having to try to do everything yourself.

You must send information in a form which its receivers can understand – it is useless to speak in French to a listener who only knows Japanese.

English now is probably closer to being a global language than any other tongue in history. But there are many senders and receivers who believe they are speaking a version of English but who do not really understand each other – and many millions who do not understand it at all.

Satellite phone technology and the Internet have made it possible to pass information rapidly to anywhere on earth or beyond. But they do not guarantee the message will be accurate or intelligible to the receiver. Senders of messages must always seek feedback from the receivers, and make honest use of it in the messages they transmit. If they do not, they will never be sure that their message has been understood and acted upon correctly, or in the right spirit.

The quality of the message and its transmission are **always** the responsibility of the sender, whatever the medium being used.

It is far easier to develop new methods of transmitting information than it is to develop the knowledge and skills of the people who use them. This workbook will help you both understand the task of communicating and develop a range of skills to help you do so effectively.

4.1 Objectives

When you have completed this workbook, you will be better able to:

- understand how important it is that there is clear communication throughout the working environment;
- recognize and overcome barriers to communication;
- select and use the method of communication which is most suited to the circumstances;
- check that messages are clearly received and understood, however they are sent;
- understand the power of non-verbal communication and take it into account when you are both sending and receiving information;
- recognize and respond to body language and behaviour.

5 Activity planner

The following activities require some planning so you may want to look at these now.

- Activity 10 on page 14 suggests that you find a colleague to whom you can read a passage of text, as part of assessing how effective it is as a verbal briefing.
- Activity 13 on page 20 asks you to prepare a briefing document on the strengths and weaknesses of communication in your own area.
- Activity 25 on page 47 asks you to look at your own job and its immediate communication needs as though with a fresh pair of eyes.
- Activity 36 on page 70 asks you to review the channels of non-verbal communication used in your workplace, and to list recommendations for making further use of this powerful and frequently under-used means of getting a message across.

Extension 4 (Session C) is a checklist which you can use to assess your own non-verbal communication and that of members of your team. You might find it useful again to discuss the results of your analysis with a trusted colleague in confidence.

The Work-based assignment asks you to follow the progress of information which you are asked to provide in the course of your job and assess its relevance and the use which is made of it, making recommendations for improvements as your analysis shows to be necessary.

Some or all of these Activities may provide the basis of evidence for your S/NVQ portfolio. All Work-based activities and the Work-based assignment are signposted with this icon.

Session A
The communication process

1 Introduction

Have you ever followed a political coup in the media? Did you notice that the first thing those involved want to do is to gain control of television and radio stations and national newspapers? Then they can control how information is communicated to foes, friends – and probably most importantly, **potential** friends who may join their side.

It's all about communication, and making communication work in your favour.

Communication is used to change public opinion, or what consumers buy. It is a large part of the activity of many organizations which employ communication directors, public relations executives and media consultants whose job, basically, is to put their organization's point of view across in the most favourable light possible.

Media studies courses are among the most popular choices for a degree, given the career opportunities that they present.

This is really nothing new. Managers of organizations at all levels have always had to communicate – with employees, customers, shareholders, suppliers. Indeed, there are often legal requirements to do so, as with the publishing of annual reports to shareholders, price lists to customers and safety notices to employees.

When we communicate with our workteam we normally want to get them to do something. It is very important though to explain **why** you want them to do things, to help gain their trust and commitment to what is needed.

So how can we communicate effectively with our teams, and what happens if we don't?

2 The importance of communicating effectively at work

1   The manager of a baker's shop rang the bakery, 40 miles away, in despair. That morning she had received 50 expensive special order products which she did not usually stock. She had specifically ordered 15 when placing her telephone order the day before. The products were perishable and most would have to be scrapped the next day.

2   A life insurance company wrote to large numbers of customers, offering new products for sale. Many of those written to had died, causing distress to their next of kin and great embarrassment to the company.

3   A company was considering closing a branch in July, with the loss of hundreds of jobs. In March, senior managers at a sister company supplying raw materials were told of this in confidence so that they could make contingency plans for delivery routes. The sister company's drivers were told – again in confidence – to avoid potential trouble with them later on. One driver was related to an employee at the threatened branch, whom he warned. The news soon became public and caused much anguish among staff who were unsure whether their jobs would really be going.

4   A factory manager planned an expensive emergency evacuation drill for the following Friday, telling only departmental managers. They had to organize essential staff to stay at their posts for safety reasons and to avoid product wastage. On the day, staff from a key department did not emerge from the factory. Its manager had not been given the list of essential staff and had decided that all 40 staff were essential. This made the whole drill a failure, and it had to be repeated at considerable cost.

I expect these four events have set you thinking of similar failures in communication from your own experience. You can see that poor communication can lead to confusion, distress, mistrust, wasted time, extra expense and bad publicity.

2.1 Why does communication fail?

In these four cases, lots of things went wrong.

Activity 1 · 3 mins

Look at each case in turn and decide whether you think it involved:

- the wrong message;
- the wrong communication method;
- the wrong audience;
- a failure to send the message at all;
- some combination of these factors. Underline your choices.

1	**Baker's shop**:	wrong message	wrong method	wrong audience	no message
2	**Insurance company**:	wrong message	wrong method	wrong audience	no message
3	**Factory closure**:	wrong message	wrong method	wrong audience	no message
4	**Evacuation drill**:	wrong message	wrong method	wrong audience	no message

See if your analysis agrees with mine.

1 The baker's shop. The wrong message got through, but perhaps the wrong method was used too. It might have been better to use a faxed order to avoid misunderstandings over special orders.

2 The insurance company. This was definitely the wrong message to send out without checking thoroughly that the recipients were suitable people to receive it. So you might add 'wrong audience'.

3 The factory closure. This was surely the wrong way to do things and the message was given to the wrong audience.

4 The evacuation drill. The message about who were to be regarded as essential staff was not sent at all.

Where the wrong message arrives, we can apply a useful acronym with which you may well be familiar.

Activity 2

2 mins

Try to expand the following set of initials into a well known phrase, used about communication systems in general and computer-based systems in particular, for when the wrong message is sent.

'GIGO' – is an abbreviation for:

G _____

I _____

G _____

O _____

The phrase I was looking for was 'Garbage In, Garbage Out'. It means that if your message is rubbish then its effect will be rubbish, and if the message itself is wrong, then you won't achieve your objective by sending it.

2.2 Spinning a yarn

We have all heard of spin doctors, people who put more emphasis on the **style** of a communication than its **content**. Very often, the aim of 'spin' is **non** communication: suppressing or obscuring the truth with a smokescreen between the audience and the actual facts.

2.3 Communicating in organizations

A good principle to keep in mind is the ABC of business communication:

Accuracy
Brevity
Clarity

for **all** communication, whatever medium you have chosen to use.

In our day-to-day work, the spin doctor approach would lead to utter disaster. For we need to ensure that:

■ people are told clearly what is required of them;
■ they are given all the information they need;
■ they have the chance to clarify anything which they have not understood fully.

Communication gets more difficult the more people you have to communicate with.

Activity 3

2 mins

Think for a moment about three teams which:

■ you currently lead, or have led; or
■ you have been a part of.

How many people were in each team?

Team 1 _____

Team 2 _____

Team 3 _____

Did the size of the team have a positive or a negative influence on communication with the team leader?

Team 1   Positive/negative

Team 2   Positive/negative

Team 3   Positive/negative

No matter how good a first line manager may be as a communicator, there is only so much time available; and if the team becomes too big – say 12 or more – effective communication will become difficult and eventually impossible.

You probably noticed that the larger the team, the more negative the effect on the quality of communication which you received or were able to give. Why is this?

If the manager communicates with all the team together, the more people there are, the harder it is to be heard clearly, the more chance there is for misunderstanding and the less time there is for the leader to deal with individual queries or misunderstandings. If team members are interested and involved, it becomes difficult to control the length of the briefing, and team members get frustrated that they cannot make the contribution they wish to.

Alternatively the manager could communicate individually with every team member, giving them each say five minutes in an eight hour working day. But:

■ for a team of 5, this would occupy 25 minutes – 5% of the working day;
■ for a team of 10, it would occupy 50 minutes – 10% of the working day;
■ for a team of 20, it would occupy 100 minutes – 20% of the working day.

That's **before** the manager has done anything else!

Most organizations, however big their staff, sub-divide the workforce into units which are manageable, that is **practical** for the manager to **communicate** with.

They have found that the best size of team with which managers can communicate is about ten or twelve. Above that, they need to sub-divide the team.

3 The communication cycle

I expect that you have dealt with plenty of processes in your time as a first line manager. A process is anything that can be broken down into:

INPUTS → PROCESS/TRANSFORMATION → OUTPUTS

There is then feedback from the process and the outputs which affect the next set of inputs.

Communication is a process like any other, except that the input is information.

We call it the communication cycle, because you can enter it at any point. And there are certain stages to that communication itself:

SENDER → ENCODING → TRANSMISSION → DECODING → RECEIVER

First of all, let's look at the inputs which the **sender** receives.

3.1 Inputs to the communication process

What you put in depends on where you work.

- If you work for an insurance company, there may be **enquiries** about insurance rates for cars or houses.
- An accounts department will receive various **documents** (invoices, credit notes, etc.).
- A trade union office will get **complaints** about working conditions or rates of pay or likely sources of friction with management.

Activity 4

List the top four regular inputs of information that arrive at your workstation. Include information received through any of the communication media you use, but exclude junk mail requiring no action.

1 _____

2 _____

3 _____

4 _____

What you listed will depend on where you work. I had a look in my various in-trays and found:

■ invoices from suppliers waiting to be paid;
■ an emailed query from a customer wanting confirmation of a deadline;
■ requests from staff for holiday;
■ a VAT return.

Any organization will be bombarded with information:

■ from central and local government, and government departments like Customs & Excise;
■ about the markets they operate in, and perhaps from a trade association;
■ from current and potential suppliers;
■ from customers − orders, payments, complaints, requests for information.

3.2 Processing information received

Just as for your own area, someone must check the information and make a decision about what to do with it. This could be:

■ to do nothing, because no action is presently required;
■ to take action yourself;
■ to get other people to take action on your behalf − in which case, you must communicate that need to those other people.

Activity 5

3 mins

Take the four sources of information from Activity 4 and decide which of the three decisions is normally appropriate for them. Underline your choices.

1	No action required	Take action myself	Act through others
2	No action required	Take action myself	Act through others
3	No action required	Take action myself	Act through others
4	No action required	Take action myself	Act through others

As a manager, you probably underlined 'Act through others' at least half of the time. Which makes you a sender – or transmitter – of information as a critical part of your job at all times.

3.3 Encoding information

When you need to transmit information to other people, you must decide how they will be best able to understand it. For example, if you work in an export department and have to communicate with a non-English speaker in Spain, it will be pointless to send a message in anything other than Spanish unless:

- you can do so in some other recognized language, such as mathematical or musical notation, which is understood throughout the world;
- you know the customer has a translator – or 'decoder' – available.

All human languages – English, Spanish, Punjabi, whatever – are ways of **encoding** a message into a form which both the sender and the receiver can understand, provided that both have learned the language.

Activity 6

2 mins

Apart from human languages, can you think of any other ways of encoding information that is to be transmitted?

1 _____

2 _____

3 _____

4 _____

You may have listed items such as Morse code; computer languages; text message codes; sign language; semaphore; railway signals (combinations of lights); chemical notation (for example H_2SO_4 for sulphuric acid). You may even have mentioned jargon, the language that people 'in the know' use to communicate with each other – and which to an outsider is both unintelligible and isolating.

All these codes have the drawback that only certain people can decode them. Take text messages. In this, standard words are reduced to a code, often changing 'you' to 'U', 'to' to '2' and 'thousand' to 'K' (for 'Kilo'). But there is no recognized universal code, and some of the abbreviations are not as obvious as the ones quoted. So if you use text messages to communicate for work, you have to make sure that you are using the same version of the code as the receiver, otherwise there is a very good chance that misunderstandings will arise.

3.4 Sending or transmitting information

There are so many means of communication available to a manager – how do you choose the right one for your particular purpose?

Activity 7

3 mins

Think about the communication in Activity 5 that you decided you had to take action on.

List up to four factors that you might need to take into account. Think about the language (or 'code'), and whether speed is essential for contacting a customer.

I thought about my customer's query about a deadline and decided that I had to answer it quickly, so I would use email as a fast but permanent record. I researched the query and found that I had to confirm a date. Since my customer is American, I didn't write '09/01/2003', because I knew that they would 'decode' that as 1 September 2003. Instead, I spelled it out as 9 January 2003.

Factors to consider:

1 _____

2 _____

3 _____

4 _____

The Data Protection Act 1998 lays down rules about the storage and retrieval of personal information held on computer systems.

If you think you could be affected by it, you should seek advice from your manager or the designated 'data controller' for your site.

You may have included:

■ speed of transmission;
■ security/confidentiality (faxes, letters or emails may be read by the wrong people);
■ efficiency – it may be more efficient to give the whole team a standard message at the same time than go through it with them individually;
■ cost – phone calls can be very expensive compared to post;
■ intelligibility – a complex product specification might be better in writing than by phone, giving the receiver more time to study it;
■ reliability;
■ personal nature – some matters are confidential but may be made known to a limited range of designated personnel, but other matters, such as appraisal data and personnel records, should be treated as personal and normally discussed only with the individual concerned.

3.5 Decoding and receiving

You may need to check that information has been received and decoded (understood):

■ fax machines usually confirm the receiving number and number of pages sent;
■ post offices can provide proof of posting or guaranteed delivery;
■ for phone messages and verbal briefings, you will need to check understanding – of which more in Session B.

4 Recognizing and overcoming barriers to communication

Every human being both needs – and wishes – to communicate with other human beings. After all, solitary confinement is one of the most severe of all punishments.

But why is it so difficult to do? Should it not come naturally, like breathing?

4.1 Non-verbal communication and body language

The problem often is that we don't just use verbal or written language – we also use other forms of code to transmit information.

We will look in Session C at non-verbal communication and body language, which are simple, powerful and effective forms of communication. To some extent, they are involuntary and so really do come as naturally as breathing.

But though these are powerful and effective, they lack subtlety and the ability to convey much in the way of detail.

Activity 8 · 2 mins

Imagine you are in a meeting with your new line manager. After about ten minutes, he becomes fidgety, sweaty and lacking in concentration. Nothing that he says gives you any cause for concern, so how do you interpret his body language?

_____

_____

_____

Well, how you interpret it depends largely on you. If you are already feeling anxious about the change of manager then you may interpret it that he is nervous about having to give you some bad news. Or you may just think he is unwell, or has remembered something he has forgotten to do, or is late for his next meeting.

You are concerned, but have no further detail to go on.

4.2 Verbal and written communication

And of course even conscious language is full of ambiguities and depends on the ability and willingness of both parties to 'speak the same language'.

Because of these factors, we encounter what we call 'barriers to communication'.

Activity 9 · 5 mins

Drawing on your own experience as a communicator **and** receiver of information, try to think of at least three barriers to communication which you have encountered when trying to communicate with people using the spoken or written word (include telephones in your list for the spoken word).

Spoken

_____

_____

_____

_____

_____

_____

_____

Written

_____

_____

_____

_____

_____

_____

_____

Like me, you were probably spoiled for choice! See how your list compares with mine.

Spoken communication

Barriers to good spoken communication include:

- poor command of the language;
- accent – strong regional or foreign accents can make the words hard or impossible to follow;
- mispronunciation of words;
- words which sound very alike, but have different meanings – like 'fifty' and 'fifteen', 'faulty' and 'forty', 'hare' and 'hair', 'horse' and 'hoarse', 'check' and 'cheque', 'time' and 'thyme';
- words which have more than one meaning – for example, 'counter' as in 'shop', 'counter' as in 'to repulse';
- jargon – using unfamiliar words, or using words with a special meaning;
- acronyms and abbreviations – like COSHH, ROM, RAM, HACCP;
- lack of grasp of the subject;
- lack of a clear message/irrelevant content;
- using the wrong words through lack of understanding;
- stressing the wrong words, making a sentence difficult to follow;
- over-complicated or long sentences, more suited to being read than listened to;
- irritating (to the listener) tone of voice, perhaps giving a conflicting message to the words being said;
- insincerity or boredom;
- speaking too softly, too slowly, too fast, too loudly – or some combination of these;
- monotonous, sleep-inducing delivery without rhythm or emphasis;
- speaking for too long – overloading the listener with information – and/or boring repetition;
- poor concentration by listeners; inattention through fatigue or sheer lack of interest;
- distracting environment – noise, interruptions, pedestrian traffic;
- poor phone lines which crackle, break up or become crossed.

Written communication

Many of the factors on the spoken list apply to written communication as well. We can also add the following:

- illegible handwriting;
- unreadable faxes or printing;
- bad spelling and/or poor grammar, which distorts or destroys the meaning intended;
- excessive length and detail, obscuring the sense of the document;
- small print size – as with insurance policies and legal documents generally.

These are both long lists and yet they still aren't comprehensive. You may have had other items on your lists, as well as describing the same factors perhaps in a slightly different way.

Perhaps we can summarize this by saying that speakers and writers too often communicate only on their own terms, creating barriers to communication with their audience.

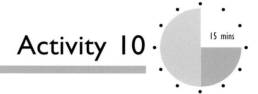

Activity 10 · 15 mins

Read the following case study and answer the questions which follow it.

Try reading it aloud too, to see how it sounds, before answering the questions. You could even read the extract to a friend or colleague to gauge their reaction to it.

Terry McCaulay is an expert on employment law and so was asked by the general manager to brief his fellow first line managers about what they needed to know about the Sex Discrimination Act. Terry took home a copy of the Act, relevant codes of practice, the company personnel manual and the employee handbook.

Here is the opening section of the talk he gave, after many hours of preparation at home. Terry read directly from notes.

'The SDA was promulgated originally in 1975 and subsequently amended by the SDA of 1986 and again by the Employment Act of 1989. Its aim was to address perceived unfairness and inequalities as to the treatment of the sexes and which had been perpetuated for many years by organisations implicitly guilty of what I might call institutional sexism. The EOC was set up to monitor the implementation of the Act and has issued a code of practice which employers can use as the basis for employment policies which are likely to be seen as good evidence of their endeavours to manage within both the letter and the spirit of the law in the event of a dispute arising. The DDA, promulgated some years later, addressed similar inequities in the disability arena and is monitored by the DDC. But that is not my subject for today's lecture. An employer is liable under the SDA and the RRA and the DDA for anything done by his or her agent or employee – that includes you and me incidentally – unless the employer can prove, possibly before an ET, that it tried to prevent the illegal act, or that it was 'ultra vires' the agent's delegated authority.'

Imagine that you were one of the audience at Terry's briefing. (You can assume that all the technical content of the briefing is factually correct.) Using the grid below, say:

1   what potential barriers to verbal communication you can identify

2   what you would have done in Terry's place to overcome the barriers you have identified.

Presentation on the Sex Discrimination Act	
Potential barrier	**How to overcome**
1	
2	
3	
4	
5	
6	

Here are some ideas.

Presentation on the Sex Discrimination Act	
Potential barrier	**How to overcome**
1 Using acronyms and abbreviations – e.g. SDA, EOC, DDC, ET	**Explain** what the abbreviation stands for – at least the **first** time it is used. And write it up on a flipchart for people to refer back to
2 Over-complicated sentences	**Read the finished briefing aloud** and see how it sounds to you. If it is hard to read, then simplify it and make each sentence shorter
3 Lack of a clear message – what is Terry trying to say which is relevant to his audience?	**Check exactly** what the brief requires. What is the target audience? What do they need to know?
4 Jargon – e.g. 'promulgated', 'institutional sexism', 'ultra vires'	**Encode only** with terms and language which you are **sure** will be readily understood by the audience – never try to impress or blind with science
5 Irrelevant content – talking about the 'DDA' and then saying it is not the topic for today	**Keep to the brief** – don't stray into topics which particularly interest **you**; keep to those which should interest **them**
6 Information overload – far too much detailed information too quickly	**Read through** the finished briefing aloud, preferably to one or two friends/colleagues, to test their reaction. Take their thoughts into account and simplify or re-position the information which is hard to comprehend

5 Ensuring effective communication in the workplace

So how can we do it better?

First, we must **want** to communicate. Secondly, we need to **understand** that **communication** is always a top priority. Managers can only get things done through other people if they:

- **state clearly** what is required of their team;
- provide all the **information** which they need to do the job;
- ensure that everyone involved has received the **same message**;
- **check** that the message has been **understood**.

One very good method is the team briefing.

5.1 Team briefing

These deal with topics which the listeners need to know or do something about. For the normal day-to-day business of management, talking directly to your team as a group is extremely effective and impossible to better.

Activity 11 · 2 mins

Think about a team briefing that you attended, as team member or manager, which sticks in your mind as having been pretty useless. Try to identify four reasons why.

_____

_____

_____

_____

You should have recognized some of the following barriers to communication:

- too many people – a manageable number is ten to twelve;
- unsuitable venue – it should be reasonably quiet and free of distractions;
- bad timing – 'little and often' is better than 'large and seldom', and it is better if they take place in official time at the beginning of a working day rather than at the end when people will be tired and less attentive;
- irrelevant and backward looking content – it should be 'what we are doing today/tomorrow/this week', not a review of the past six months' performance figures. Use past data only if it is relevant to what you want the team to do. For example, three recent near misses might require the re-routing of fork-lift truck routes;
- poor speaker – think about pace, voice level, accent, tone and quality of voice;
- no feedback – check that the message has been understood and that the listeners all have the same understanding of what has been said.

5.2 Language barriers

If some or most of your team do not speak English very well, this will present a real barrier to communication, with serious implications for issues such as quality, health, safety and welfare.

There is no straightforward answer to this, so you need to find an individual solution for the particular circumstances. You will almost certainly need help from your manager. You cannot just ignore the problem because:

- you have a responsibility to communicate with your team;
- if you employ people for whom the language is a barrier, you have to find a way to overcome it.

5.3 One-to-one communication

Communicating just with one person is appropriate where the matter is more personal, or specific to an individual's work. There is no point telling a whole team of 12 about temporary delivery arrangements for just one route because of road works.

But one-to-one communication is very ineffective for putting a common message across to a number of people: the chances are that they will all get a slightly different message and possibly do something different to what you intend. As you are not a machine, you are likely to become bored and make mistakes, or miss things out, as the individual briefings progress.

It is also a very inefficient use of your time.

Activity 12 · 2 mins

There is a story, possibly true and certainly believable, of a World War 1 general who sent a message down the line by word of mouth, using a relay of runners. All the telephone lines were destroyed. Here is the message as it reached 'base':

'Send three and fourpence, we're going to a dance.'

What do you think the general actually said to the first runner?

Your suggestion: _____

_____

You may have heard the story before and know the answer. If not, see how near you came to the answer given on page 90.

What the story illustrates is how distorted messages become when they are passed by word of mouth. The general had no choice, but you have both the means and the responsibility to communicate effectively with your team.

5.4 The 'grapevine'

This is one of the most efficient ways of spreading information, even if it is often inaccurate and distorted.

The grapevine will flourish anywhere that managers ignore their responsibility to communicate with staff. If you do not give people credible information, someone or other will invent it for themselves and feed it into the grapevine of informal communication which exists in every organization.

Of course grapevines will always exist, however well an organization is managed, as the instinct to speculate and gossip is fundamental to human beings. But it will stick to harmless gossip if people can generally rely on being well informed.

Activity 13

30 mins

S/NVQ D1.2

This Activity may provide the basis of appropriate evidence for your S/NVQ Portfolio. If you are intending to take this course of action, it might be better to write your answers on separate sheets of paper.

Design a short briefing document, no longer than ten minutes' speaking time, in which you will present to your manager your views on:

- the strengths of the communication cycle in your own organization;
- any barriers to communication that exist;
- your recommendations for improvement;
- building on the existing strengths you perceive;
- breaking down the barriers identified;
- areas where you will need help from your manager or specialist managers in the personnel or human resources department.

Aim for a short, pithy style using as few words as possible, in the form of bullet points or headings, simply to guide you through a subject which will be thoroughly familiar to you anyway.

Self-assessment 1

15 mins

1 What do you understand by the acronym 'GIGO'?

_____

2 How does the need to communicate effectively restrict the size of teams?

_____

_____

3 What is the 'communication cycle'?

_____

_____

4   What are the main stages in communication?

_____

_____

_____

_____

5   All managers must be skilled _____ because their job is about _____ done through _____ people who must be informed what is _____ of them.

6   List five barriers to verbal communication in your experience of work.

_____

_____

_____

_____

_____

7   A practical limit to the size of a group to be briefed would be:

4   8   12   16   20

Please circle your choice.

8   Name six essential features of an effective briefing.

_____

_____

_____

_____

_____

_____

9   What do you understand by the 'grapevine' and what may be its effects on communication at work?

_____

_____

10   _____ and _____ are examples of situations where _____ to _____ communication is appropriate.

11 Give six examples of barriers to effective written communication.

_____

_____

_____

_____

_____

_____

Answers to these questions can be found on pages 87–88.

6 Summary

- Communication is arguably the single most important aspect of **every** manager's job. Managers aim to achieve their objectives though other people and, to do that, they must ensure those people know what is required of them.

- There are limits to how many people a manager can communicate effectively with. Once the numbers managed exceed 12 or thereabouts, it becomes difficult – and soon impossible – to communicate effectively.

- All communication activities, human and electronic, involve receiving, decoding, processing, encoding and transmitting information within the communication cycle of inputs, processing and outputs.

- There are many barriers which obstruct the cycle, but which can be overcome by recognizing them and developing the skills to ensure that the right message is received and understood.

- Team briefing is the most effective and efficient (for time and cost) way of communicating information to working teams, to ensure that everyone gets the same message at the same time – and has the opportunity to clarify anything which they do not understand.

- If managers refuse to communicate, or do it badly or grudgingly, informal communication systems (often known as 'grapevines') will flourish.

Session B
Communication media

1 Introduction

How many ways do you receive communications in a normal day? Face-to-face, no doubt, but also phone calls, text messages, faxes and emails? Television, radio, Internet, public address? There are more ways – or media – of communicating information available now than ever before.

This should be an advantage, but there are problems in it for senders and receivers. Too much information can be as much of a problem as too little.

Because no matter how sophisticated the delivery medium and how great its capacity to deliver 24/7, there are still only 168 hours in a week – and most people need to sleep for at least 25% of them.

So, both at work and at home, people need to make informed choices about which medium to use and when to say 'no'.

The communication cycle (see Session A) applies to all media. Information is received, decoded, processed, encoded and transmitted. Some media, such as broadcasting, telephone networks and the Internet, effectively have infinite capacity to transmit data, but the people who do the processing – the makers of a feature film, for instance – do not.

The GIGO principle – garbage in, garbage out – applies to **every** medium used, including email, text messaging and the intranets which many organizations use. The more information is fed into them, the more its quality and relevance needs to be controlled.

This session will help you to select the correct medium for the information you need to communicate – from face-to-face interviews to sending a message throughout the organization and beyond.

The American Marshall McLuhan said famously that 'the medium is the message' – how you say something matters more than what you say. Sometimes you may feel this is true, but ultimately the GIGO factor will catch up with those who send messages that are worthless.

2 Choosing the right method of communication

We are spoilt for choice when it comes to media. How do we choose the right medium for our message?

2.1 Looking at the medium's effectiveness and efficiency

'Effectiveness' and 'efficiency' are often used as though they mean more or less the same thing. But, in management terms, they have very different meanings.

Activity 14   2 mins

What do you understand by these two 'e' words?

Efficiency

_____

_____

_____

Effectiveness

_____

_____

_____

I'm going to use the following definitions throughout this session; see how they compare with yours.

Efficiency is getting the greatest amount of output for the effort and resources being used.

Effectiveness is producing a desired result. It is a matter of quality as well as quantity. A desired result may not be quite the same thing as sheer amount of output, as the example below shows.

Activity 15

3 mins

Holibus operates coach holidays throughout England and is planning a new advertising campaign. Most of their customers are in their 60s or above who don't want to use their own cars. In all, Holibus wishes to take two hours of advertising on television, as a series of two-minute slots. They are offered rates for various times of day and night, and calculate that taking the off-peak slots at night could save them up to half the spend they had budgeted for.

What would you do in their position? Answer only **one** question 'YES'.

1	Choose the peak-time rates to reach a wider audience	YES/NO
2	Choose off-peak times to save money	YES/NO
3	Neither of these	YES/NO

If you choose option 3, what would you have done instead?

_____

_____

_____

_____

Let's work out the arguments for and against each option.

Option 1

YES — This will use the money more **efficiently**, because we'll reach many more people per £1 spent.

NO — It's too expensive and many of the viewers won't be our potential customers — that would be **ineffective**.

Option 2

YES — This will save us a lot of money. We could have twice as much advertising for the same price and that's **efficient**.

NO — what's the point of advertising when most of our potential customers are asleep? — that would not be **effective**.

Option 3

YES — We could use the money in other ways, like persuading existing customers to take a second holiday at a discount price. That could be more **effective** use of the money, because we know those customers already buy.

NO — because we want to reach as many people as possible with advertising. That's more **efficient** per £1 spent.

Probably, Option 3 would be the most effective use of the money, no matter how efficient TV advertising might be at reaching much larger numbers. If it didn't persuade them to buy, then it wouldn't matter how many of them had seen the ad.

For all managers, the ideal world is one in which you combine effectiveness with efficiency, that is:

you do the RIGHT thing in the BEST POSSIBLE way.

In 2002, a national recruitment campaign featuring high profile personalities and extensive TV coverage cost the Police Force £12 million. It recruited just 400 people at a cost of £30,000 each. Using local publicity the police reckon to spend usually around £250 per recruit.

Activity 16   10 mins

You find out that 20 people out of 400 who work on a site may be greatly affected by a new pedestrian route from the main gate to their laboratory. Other employees may use the new path occasionally.

The message you have to send about the path is important, and safety issues are involved.

Because of cost and time, you have to keep this ideal in mind when you are choosing between, say:

1   putting a notice on the safety and welfare notice board

2   sending an email to everyone on site

3   organizing a briefing for the people most affected by the topic.

What do you think would be the most efficient and the most effective ways of communicating about this path? Take into account the potential costs of each option as you see them, and use the grid to note the factors you believe should be considered. I've put in a 'starter' comment for each factor.

Factors	Option 1 Notice on board	Option 2 Email to everyone	Option 3 Briefing for 20 people
1	Most won't read	Many won't read	380 people not there but they may need to know
2			
3			
4			
5			
6			

My recommendation is: _____

_____

Have a look at the other factors I came up with on page 90.

I hope you can see that there is more than one way to do the job. Sometimes a combination of methods may be needed to achieve effectiveness. In this case, for simplicity, you were offered only three options, though many others would have been available, such as a letter to all employees with their next salary advice.

How did your final recommendation agree with the following approach?

1 To brief the 20 people most affected in two groups of no more than 12.

2 To put a notice on the safety notice board as a permanent reminder to **all** staff.

2.2 How to choose

Your completed grid will show some of the factors which we need to take into account when choosing the most effective channel for communication.

Ask yourself these key questions.

Key question	The answer affects the communication's:
1 Do we need to communicate at all?	effectiveness
2 Will we reach all the people who need to know?	effectiveness
3 Can people deny having been told?	effectiveness
4 How long will it last?	effectiveness
5 Can we obtain feedback?	effectiveness
6 How much will it cost?	efficiency
7 How simple is it to use?	efficiency
8 How quickly can it be done?	efficiency

Ideally, you are looking for a method of communication which:

■ reaches everyone who needs to know   = effective
■ is acknowledged by them   = effective
■ has a reasonable shelf life   = effective
■ provides confirmation of   = effective
   understanding
■ is cheap, simple and quick to use   = efficient

The eight questions will help make a decision about any communication choice, from the very simplest — perhaps informing a team that a new

The Internet makes it possible, in principle, for every person on earth to communicate with every other person.
But there is no control over what is fed into the system, so the GIGO principle warns you to beware what you may obtain from it.
And browsing the Internet can use vast amounts of time by comparison with using more focused reference sources, and be more expensive.

colleague will be arriving next Monday – to the most complex, perhaps deciding how next year's advertising budget should be spent.

The first question – do we need to communicate at all? – is the most important of all. If the answer is 'no', then there is no point in going any further and spending anything (money or time) doing something which is unnecessary.

2.3 Who to choose

Next we need to ask ourselves 'Will we reach all the people who need to know?'

This is tricky. We might make the judgement that Mr X doesn't need to know, and not communicate. If, in fact, he did need to know, we have failed in our objective of communicating effectively.

> A normal person will read at between 200 and 250 words per minute, assuming a familiar subject and clearly expressed content. So a 1,000 word memo will probably take four to five minutes, assuming no distractions. That doesn't sound so long – but what if there are the equivalent of 20 per day to be read?

But if indeed he didn't need to know, then we have gone a small way towards saving the enormous sums that are spent each year on needless communications and the effects of information overload. This is especially true of emails, which take up so much of our time.

As a manager, you have a duty to make the most effective use of all the resources which you have been given responsibility for, including communication resources.

Next we need to make the big decision – which channel of communication to use.

2.4 What to choose from

The choice open to us is huge, from long-standing systems to newer and more powerful electronic ones.

Activity 17

Think about what channels are available and what groups of people they are likely to be used for in your organization. Then, in the grid provided, list the various channels of communication used either directly by you or to you or by your organization as a whole.

Place a tick against each channel that is relevant for customers, employees, suppliers and the media.

Channels used	Target Audience			
	Customers	Employees	Suppliers	The media

On page 91 you will find a grid completed with a large organization in mind, such as a supplier of products to multiple retailers with many sites around the country.

In fact, all or most of them are available to an organization of any size without excessive cost, though some of them may be unnecessary, and many are misused frequently.

Activity 18

I've grouped the various channels from Activity 17 into categories, for convenience.

Referring to the key questions 3–8 on page 30, and your own experience, how would you rate the strengths and weaknesses of each category, from Low to Medium to High? Complete the grid provided.

Channel	Certainty	Perman-ence	Feedback available	Economy	Simplicity in use	Speed of use
Oral						
Written						
Visual						
Telephonic						
Electronic						

Communication Channels — General Advantages and Disadvantages

You will find a completed grid in the Answers to activities section on page 91.

2.5 The perfect communication solution

Ideally, you would be looking for a channel which rated high in every category, one which was certain to get through, permanent, provided feedback to check understanding, and was economical, simple and quick to use.

In real life, there is no such perfect channel, so you will be looking for a workable compromise in all but the simplest situations.

The completed grid is not therefore a model which you can apply to any situation, nor does your version have to correspond to it to be right, for there is no right answer applicable to all situations.

But what you do need to do is choose the right communication channel objectively for a particular purpose, weighing the pros and cons of each before **automatically** picking up the phone, sending an email, calling a team briefing – whatever your instinctive preference may be.

Activity 19 · 5 mins

Look at the following six practical situations and state what you believe would be the right solution to the communication problems they pose.

1   One of your delivery vehicles has had an accident and you need to advise customers that their deliveries will be affected.

_____

2   You are working on a new quality manual and your boss wants to eliminate as much paper as possible.

_____

3   You need to send a complicated draft mortgage offer to a client.

_____

4   You need to bring your team up-to-date concerning three serious near misses which have happened recently.

_____

5   You need to check if seven people from other sites and departments can attend a sales meeting in three days' time.

_____

6   Contractors' employees have been using the staff restaurant and cloakrooms without authorization.

_____

You will find a series of suggestions on page 92, with a short explanation of why they were chosen.

No doubt your own recommendations range widely, as mine do, across the available channels, to suit the needs of the situation you are in.

Though your answers may differ to some extent, what really matters is the **decision-making process** which you have gone through, based on the activities in this session, your own experience and the resources available to you.

3 Face-to-face communication

There is one kind of communication which does come naturally to virtually everyone, almost like breathing, so why does anyone need to think about how they do it?

It is perhaps because people often don't recognize the difference between:

- a friendly conversation – which does not have to achieve any particular objective; and
- a business communication, which **does**.

In journalism, the standard rule used is:

tell them what you are going to tell them (Introduction)

tell them in as few words as you can (Content)

tell them what you've told them (Summary)

You will find that all news broadcasts follow this simple, effective plan.

Friendly conversations are essential to getting to know more about your team and building good relationships within it, but there are many occasions for which a more formal structure is required. You will earn respect from your team if they know that you will create a businesslike, purposeful atmosphere when the object of the communication is to get things done as a result of it.

Many people – and you may be one of them – actually resent having their time wasted going down 'blind alleys', with irrelevant subjects or the constant repetition of things which they know about already.

People also forget, or ignore, the basic principle of communication, which is that it is a cycle, with information flowing in more than one direction – or at least **needing** to flow in more than one direction.

3.1 A structure for effective face-to-face communication

The following approach has been tried and tested in many circumstances and over many generations.

Stage	Comments
1 Decide what you want to achieve	Is this a briefing meeting, a counselling session, a disciplinary hearing? The facts required will differ widely.
2 Gather your materials	These must relate directly to your objective.
3 Arrange them into a logical flow – with a clear beginning, middle and end. Decide how you can persuade your listeners to do what you require willingly.	Think it through carefully from the **listeners**' perspective – if they already know the content, why are you talking to them?
4 Tailor the pitch of your language to suit your listeners.	This will be different as between, say, new recruits and experienced employees who know any jargon you may use as shorthand.
5 Anticipate objections and counter-arguments which may arise. If you tell people **why** you need them to do something they are far more likely to co-operate.	Forewarned is forearmed – if you are dealing with a tricky subject, like poor performance, you need to think through the defensive reactions you may receive.
6 Decide what advice and/or feedback you are looking for.	You don't have to be the fount of all wisdom – teams should contribute to their own self-improvement, and communication is most effective when it works two ways.
7 Plan a summary or conclusion which will leave your listener knowing what they need to know – and committed to whatever actions may be required.	On the basis of 'if you go away knowing nothing else – be sure to remember this'. If you are looking for improved performance, your audience must want to do it for you.
8 If possible, practise beforehand with a friendly listener.	Try not to go through your learning curve at the expense of your audience, whatever its size.

3.2 Passive listening

Now, let's look at the other aspect of face-to-face communication: listening.

Did you know that human beings speak at around 125 words per minute, but can **think** at 600 words per minute or more?

That's four times as fast — so there should be no problem. But frequently, there is.

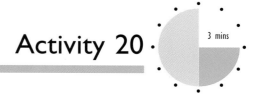

Activity 20

3 mins

Write down as many symptoms as you can think of for people who are bad listeners. Concentrate on matters which are within the **listener's** control, so exclude:

- environmental factors. No one can listen to a briefing when standing next to a pneumatic drill — but they can try to ensure they get enough sleep and so don't fall asleep;
- faults which lie with the speaker — such as mumbling or rambling delivery.

Aim for about six reasons, based on your own experience.

_____

_____

_____

_____

_____

_____

_____

_____

_____

_____

_____

'I hear what you say' has become a meaningless and often offensive phrase. Because it has been said so often by people who have no intention whatever of taking any notice of what they have heard.

I expect your list looks something like mine:

1   assuming the subject is boring beforehand – and so 'switching off' before the unfortunate speaker has begun;

2   ignoring the **content** of what is being said and just attacking the **way** it is delivered in a nit picking fashion which gives no chance for a fair hearing;

3   frequent interrupting – which is really a sign of wishing to dominate the proceedings and 'put down' the speaker;

4   going to sleep – through lack of concentration or fatigue brought on by too little sleep;

5   closing the mind to technical or awkward topics;

6   day dreaming;

7   picking fights – latching onto a word like 'poor' (as in performance) or 'unacceptable' (as in standards) in the 'what do you mean by that' aggressive mode;

8   listening selectively – usually to only what is of interest, like a specialist subject, or represents good news, like bonus payments.

Do you recognize any of the symptoms in yourself? If you do, then you are in very good company – for while **listening** comes naturally to human beings and requires no effort, **hearing** requires positive effort.

> Lip reading has been used in mills, factories and other noisy environments over many years. Many hearing people have become proficient lip readers – proving the value of **looking at the speaker** to improve their listening.

3.3   Active hearing

If you can recognize the symptoms, you should be in with a good chance of finding a cure.

Activity 21

5 mins

Think of some simple ways in which people showing the symptoms identified above can cure them – and so move from **passive** listening to **active hearing**.

Take each of the eight symptoms in turn. Begin each sentence 'They should try to . . . '. I've completed Number 1, to get you started.

1   They should try to . . . have an open mind and let the speaker convince them that the topic is interesting.

2   _____

_____

3   _____

_____

4   _____

_____

5   _____

_____

6   _____

_____

7   _____

_____

8   _____

_____

You will find some suggestions in the 'Answers to activities' section on page 92.

Of them all, the single most important for most poor listeners is simply to look at the speaker, cutting out any visual distractions.

4 Gathering and using feedback

When you are the sender of the information, you need to know that you have been understood. This is especially important with verbal communication when the receiver has nothing to refer to when you have finished.

You do this by asking questions and being an active hearer of answers to the questions you have asked. Because if you don't listen, it doesn't really make any difference how polished your questioning techniques are.

But there are some other things you can do as well to get the feedback you need.

4.1 Observation

In face-to-face communication you can see the person or people you are addressing. Just as they should focus on you to improve their active hearing, so should you observe their reactions to what you are saying.

Activity 22 · 4 mins

Picture the following scenes and ask yourself what feedback the speaker is receiving, without anybody saying a word. Jot down your thoughts.

Marita was briefing her shop staff about changes to delivery arrangements beginning the following week. There were five women listening. One looked stony faced throughout; another shook her head every so often; the third looked down at her feet; the fourth, who was a new starter, was evidently concentrating hard; and the fifth occasionally clicked her teeth, or drew in her breath.

Your thoughts:

_____

_____

_____

Sean was talking to the stablehands in the racing stable where he worked. He had just heard from the trainer that an important owner was going to place ten good horses with them next season. Six staff were present. One was smiling broadly; the second nodded frequently; the third – known to be work-shy – looked dubious; another made a 'thumbs up' signal; one – famously emotional about 'his' horses – was almost in tears; and the sixth, who had just married, opened a wallet and gestured as though putting money in it.

Your thoughts:

_____

_____

_____

Did your thoughts run along the same lines as mine?

Marita was evidently giving unwelcome news, perhaps because her staff (other than the new recruit) simply don't like change – or they fear the new arrangements will alter the service they give to customers. If Marita was looking around her team as she spoke, she would have picked up the signals of doubt and disagreement without anything being said.

Sean had very good news to impart – except to the work-shy lad. New, good horses are a boost for morale, and would only be placed with them because they are thought to be a good operation. Also, there is a chance of more prize money and improved job security. No wonder that most of the team looked so happy about it – something that Sean would see if he looked around them as he spoke.

These are examples of feedback coming from interpreting body language and non-verbal communication, which we will look at fully in Session C.

Note for now what an immediate and powerful way observation is of obtaining feedback from face-to-face communication.

4.2 Knowing your people

In both the scenes pictured above it was implied that the managers **knew** their people as individuals – who was work-shy, who loved the job, who was a new starter, who needed more money.

This is important when interpreting their reactions because:

- some people can look miserable even when they are perfectly happy;
- others try never to show emotion of any kind;
- others seem to look perpetually cheerful, whatever the situation.

If you don't **know** them as people, you won't be able to allow for these idiosyncrasies and may misinterpret what you see.

4.3 Asking questions

You will get more precise feedback by asking questions, as Mick is trying to do here.

Activity 23 · 2 mins

Mick has just given a ten-minute briefing on bank holiday working arrangements in the warehouse. He looks around the team and says:

'Everyone OK about that, taken it all in all right?'

There were a few nods and grunts and Mick said:

'Good, let's all get back to work then.'

How much feedback do you think he has obtained from the question posed?

_____

_____

_____

You probably answered 'none' or 'very little' – or words to that effect. The question he asked was a closed one – inviting a yes/no answer. In fact questions in that form – the 'Everyone happy so far?' kind – do not invite feedback of any sort, even an honest 'no!'

Closed questions cut short discussion and are not helpful if you want to check people's understanding, or reactions, either emotional or reasoned, to what you have said.

But they are useful for confirming what has been heard and for keeping control of the length of a discussion, as in:

'Have we covered everything you needed to know about the new arrangements?'

Mick would have found out much more by asking open questions, for example as follows, where he has briefed the staff on working arrangements which are both complicated and unwelcome, at least to some staff.

- **How** do you think this will work out in practice for the drivers?
- **What** differences can you see from last year?
- **Which** change do you think will cause most problems?
- **Where** do you reckon most of the drivers will be on the day before Christmas Eve?
- **When** do you want me to go through the final details?
- **Who** is likely to make a fuss among the customers?
- **Why** do you think we've had to make the changes this year?

All these open questions invite people to talk and say what they think.

Mick may not always like what he hears, but at least he will find out what problems and misgivings there are. Then he will have the chance to do something about them in the immediate future.

4.4 Using feedback

What do you do with feedback once you've got it? It depends.

- You may simply need to clarify something which the listener misheard.
- You may need to make changes to the plan you were describing, because the feedback shows it needs improvement.
- You may have to emphasize that the understanding is correct and that the plan will go ahead as described, despite the reservations people have. None of us gets everything we want all the time.

4.5 Telephone and other 'remote' verbal communication

Many misunderstandings arise because speakers and receivers don't check that they have both have the **same** message.

You can easily check that you have, by asking the other person to repeat back anything which could be misheard. Many words and names sound similar, which can lead to serious mistakes.

EXTENSION I
This is the standard phonetic alphabet, especially useful over telephones, walkie talkies and radio – or where the quality of line is often poor.
The standard phonetic alphabet is recognized internationally.

Numbers particularly need to be carefully checked, ideally by reading as a series of digits: '19' becomes 'one nine', and '90' becomes 'nine zero' to avoid confusion between them.

One standard way of avoiding errors is to use the **standard phonetic alphabet**, which assigns a word to each letter of the alphabet. A becomes 'Alpha', B is 'Bravo', C is 'Charlie', and so on. This avoids the listener mistaking 'M' for 'N', for example.

5 Non-verbal communication

Let's go back now to a subject that we saw briefly in Session A – communication which takes place without language, i.e. 'body language' or 'non-verbal communication'. When should a manager pay attention to this?

The short answer is: always. We all register and interpret such behaviour all the time, it comes naturally. But acting on it is another matter.

5.1 Receiving non-verbal communication

Sometimes a straightforward instruction must be issued. The only feedback required is to see evidence that the instruction has been carried out.

A very good example of this is an emergency situation, such as an evacuation for fire or an accident about to happen in a warehouse.

Say a person is about to drive a forklift into someone whom they cannot see from their cab.

- There is no time for a discussion.
- The people involved should have been trained **beforehand** in the procedures.
- They must know what to do – obey the instruction – and trust the person giving the instruction.

As a manager, you have to develop enough trust in your team members so that they know to react appropriately, that you are not just throwing your weight around. And a good tip is to use an 'order' tone only when circumstances justify it.

5.2 Giving information in non-verbal form

We covered how you receive non-verbal communication in section 4.1 *Observation*. What about using it to **give** information to members of your team, or to other people affected by what they are doing?

Activity 24 · 3 mins

Can you list four situations when it would be appropriate and necessary for you to use non-verbal means of sending a message to your team or a member of it? Think of a means of communication you could use employing the senses of touch, sight, smell and taste.

Touch _____

_____

Sight _____

_____

Smell _____

_____

Taste _____

_____

Political cartoonists go to the root of a complex situation with a simple, readily understood cartoon. They prove a picture can be worth a thousand words or more.

Other forms of non-verbal communication are just as powerful.

45

I found it harder to find examples of using smell and taste, but these are the ones I came up with.

Touch – Taking someone's arm to prevent their walking into some danger where there was no time to shout a warning. If you have team members with poor vision, you may need to use such tactile signals for various purposes, especially where safety is concerned.

Sight – Hand signals are used in many situations where noise or distance make a verbal communication inaudible, or too slow to interpret. Signals are used for directing vehicles, showing how a heavy load is to be manoeuvred safely, showing approval or the reverse with the well known 'thumbs up' or 'thumbs down' signals. Colours are introduced sometimes as warnings. For example, food not fit for human consumption is often marked blue – a rare colour to find in human food.

Smell – A distinctive smell was introduced into odourless gas supplies to warn householders and gas fitters of the presence of gas – a safer way of finding out than by lighting a match.

Taste – A poisonous but innocuous-tasting substance could be given a nasty flavour to deter consumption (by animals as well as people).

5.3 Interpreting the signals

For communication to be effective, both the sender and receiver need to interpret them in the same way. For example, crane drivers use a simple code which everyone working on a dock is trained to use, leaving no room for misunderstanding.

Otherwise, you are in the same position as two speakers, one of them using Japanese and the other responding in Gaelic. For example:

- though a shake of the head means 'no' and a nod means 'yes' to most western Europeans, you just may be observing people for whom the signals are **reversed** or meaningless;
- there's no point introducing a distinctive smell into a gas unless the people receiving the smell signal know why it is there;
- some people cannot distinguish between some colours – so the blue colouration introduced into meat may need supplementing with another warning signal, like an unappetising smell or a written warning.

We will look further at the strengths, subtleties and shortcomings of non-verbal communication and body language in the next session.

Remember always that non-verbal forms of communication can be just as open to misinterpretation as verbal ones. Be aware of their pitfalls as well as their power and immediacy.

Activity 25 · 30 mins

S/NVQ D1.2

This Activity may provide the basis of appropriate evidence for your S/NVQ portfolio. If you are intending to take this course of action, you might find it helpful to record your notes on separate sheets of paper.

Look at the job which you are now doing as though it were a new role to you and you were looking at it with a fresh pair of eyes.

Record up to six major communication needs you have.

- State what means of communication are used now.
- If you are happy with them, explain why.
- If you are not happy with them, recommend what you would use instead and why it would be more effective.

You may find the work you did in Activity 17 helpful in assessing the strengths and weaknesses of each possible method.

Here are some ideas to get you started. Think about:

- internal needs, such as briefing, training and reviewing performance;
- external communication with customers, neighbours and outside organizations;
- any contractors who work in your area, but are not employed directly by your organization.

Review of Communication Methods		
Communication need	Current method	Recommended method
1		
2		
3		
4		
5		
6		

Self-assessment 2

10 mins

1 The best option to use for any communication is the one which combines _____ with _____.

2 The _____ alphabet is an _____ recognized system for _____ that oral messages are received _____.

3 What are the seventh and eighth questions from the list of eight key questions to ask when assessing methods of communication?

■ (7)

■ (8)

4 What do you understand by 'information overload'?

_____

_____

5 The journalist's rule about communication begins with 'Tell them what you are going to tell them.' How does it go on?

_____

6 List the words with which 'open' questions begin. What in general are they useful for doing?

_____

_____

7 Why is it important to obtain feedback for most of the communication which you send?

_____

_____

8 Give two examples of the proper use of 'closed' questions which invite a yes/ no answer.

_____

_____

9   Name two possible situations in which you may need to communicate with someone without seeking verbal feedback.

_____

_____

Answers to these questions can be found on pages 88–89.

6 Summary

■ The first question to ask is 'Do I need to communicate at all?' If the answer is 'no', then why not stop there?

■ Applying the 'need to know' principle sensibly can save people being flooded with information they do not need – such as emails, memos, adverts for products they never buy or briefing information which is irrelevant to them.

■ The means of communication available to you can make use of all the senses which people possess, i.e. sight, hearing, touch, taste and smell.

■ In practice, people rely rather too heavily on the spoken word, which is often unreliable and prone to misinterpretation.

■ Non-verbal communication and body language often give a far more accurate picture of the real messages being transmitted and received than what is actually said.

■ There are any number of delivery systems, ranging from direct, face-to-face interviews through to tannoys, telephones, faxes and the Internet or intranet.

■ There is no one means of communication which is right for all purposes, 'fastest' does not always mean 'best' – it depends on the need.

■ For every communication need identified, decide what the most effective means will be to put the message across – there's no point using the cheapest if the message won't get through.

  ■ Do we need to communicate at all?
  ■ Will we reach all the people who need to know?
  ■ Can people deny having been told?
  ■ How long will it last?
  ■ Can we obtain feedback?
  ■ How much will it cost?
  ■ How simple is it to use?
  ■ How quickly can it be done?

■ Plan what you intend to communicate beforehand, just as you plan every other business activity.

■ Assess the feedback you receive for any communication, both verbal and non-verbal, and take any appropriate actions arising from it – including any improvements you need to make to your own skills as a communicator.

Session C
Non-verbal communication

1 Introduction

We possess five senses and we receive information by means of all of them. They are:

- hearing;
- sight;
- touch;
- smell;
- taste – which is closely linked to smell.

We get so much workplace information verbally and in writing that we could be forgiven for believing these are the most important channels, but that is not true.

Long before they learned to speak or to write, our ancestors developed ways of communicating through physical signals and signs, as other animals did – and still do. We recognize and respond to those signals instinctively and immediately now in the computer age, just as they did in every age before us.

Conscious language, spoken and written, can convey much subtle and detailed information. But, because it is used consciously, it can just as well be used to conceal what the sender really thinks and feels, rather than to express it.

In fact, if people really said (or wrote) exactly what they felt and thought all the time, the likely result would be conflict, or utter chaos!

Think for a moment. How many times have you concealed your real thoughts and emotions with moderate, inexpressive language?

How would your team react if you always said exactly what you felt about their performance or attitude? And have you sometimes been surprised when they have 'seen through' you, and spotted what was really going on?

What may have spoiled your cover are the unconscious signals that you gave to the receiver, especially in face-to-face situations. Managers need to recognize and control their own body language, and influence the body language of other people, as a key interpersonal skill at work.

2 Understanding different types of body language

EXTENSION 2
If you want to find out more about *Body Language at Work*, try this authoritative and reasonably priced book.

'Just look at his body language – there's no chance of winning now.'

How many times have you heard sports commentators say this about tennis players or boxers? Body language is a topic that crops up in many areas of life, but is it just idle chatter, or can you really tell anything from observing the unconscious or conscious behaviour of people?

2.1 The negative . . .

Activity 26

3 mins

Look at the list of emotional states which follow and suggest how you might recognize them, not from what people **say**, but from how they **behave**:

Fear

_____

Depression

_____

Anger

_____

Disappointment

_____

Boredom

_____

Puzzlement

_____

Your answer may differ somewhat from mine, but I expect it will be pretty similar in most respects.

■ **Fear** is indicated by shrinking or cowering away, protecting the face with an arm or even rolling up into a ball as a hedgehog does.

■ **Depression** is shown by a bowed head, downcast eyes, a shuffling gait when walking.

■ **Anger** is displayed through staring eyes, clenched fists, tightened lips, clenched teeth and heightened colour. Approaching in a menacing fashion or standing over someone.

■ **Disappointment** is evidenced through dismal gestures of the hands and arms, shrugging of the shoulders, raising the eyes above, turning away.

- **Boredom** is indicated by yawning, looking about for something more interesting, doodling, clock watching, drumming the fingers – ultimately walking out of the situation.

- **Puzzlement** is shown by puckered brows, facial muscles tightened by the effort to concentrate, shaking of the head; stroking of the chin with the hand.

I've taken more than 100 words to describe those six states, but you would recognize them instantly from observing people exhibiting them.

All these emotions tend to be rather negative, though puzzlement can be a perfectly healthy state when tackling an interesting task.

2.2 . . . and the positive

What about more positive emotions, then? Do you need people to describe them to you, or can you recognize them just by looking?

Activity 27 · 3 mins

Look at this list and describe the behaviour you associate with them:

Joy

_____

Success

_____

Achievement

_____

Determination

_____

Enlightenment

_____

Congratulation

_____

Again, you may differ a little from my suggestions, but you will probably agree broadly with them.

- Even adults may literally 'jump for **joy'**, forgetful for a moment of the normal constraints about showing their feelings. Broad smiles, and looking about to find people to include in their happiness, are all the order of the day.

- **Success** may be shown by a thumbs up sign, raising the arms above the head.

- **Achievement** may show itself in a nodding of the head ('I've got it!'), or a slight smile.

- **Determination** is shown by jutting out the chin, tightening the facial muscles, fixing the gaze on the object to be achieved.

- **Enlightenment** is indicated by a slow nod of the head, eyes gradually opening more widely, a relaxation of the facial muscles.

- **Congratulation** may include clapping another person on the back, shaking one or more hands warmly or even hugging or kissing the object of congratulation. Self-congratulation might include placing the hands together and shaking them slowly, vigorous nodding of the head ('yes, I've **done** it!').

Detailed surveys have shown that

More than half the communication which a human being receives is by way of body language.

Less than half is through verbal communication.

Notice it took another torrent of words to describe those six more positive emotions – this time more than 150.

2.3   The trouble with words

Actually some of the words we defined in the last two activities did not describe precisely the emotional states. You can easily mix up success with achievement, or depression with disappointment.

The positive side is that words can convey so many subtleties of expression and meaning, like the colours on an artist's palette, but the down side is that meanings of words can shade into each other. They end up meaning different things to different people, and so communicate nothing.

Former US President Bill Clinton famously answered a difficult question by saying: 'It depends how you define 'is''.

Other problems with speech are as follows.

- It takes quite a long time to convey ideas through speech and for the receiver to interpret them.
- Speech does not carry over long distances unless amplified.
- Speech can be distorted or blotted out by background noise, or carried away on the wind.

2.4 Non-verbal communication is simple

Non-verbal communication, whether voluntary or unconscious, is immediate and clear where, in situations of urgency or confusion, speech is too complex. Think of the effect of a hand raised to halt a lorry half a mile away, or a person behind a window gesturing for someone outside to come in quick.

Or is it? Well, usually it is, but there can be room for both misinterpretation and deliberate misleading.

Activity 28 · 2 mins

Nicholas, a producer of training videos, was asked to show a new induction programme, lasting around 18 minutes, to a director of his client's company. He had never met the person before and after a brief 'hello', they settled down to watch – together with the personnel manager who had actually commissioned the work.

The director watched intently throughout, said nothing but shook his head every so often. Otherwise, his face was without expression, so far as Nicholas could tell.

What do you think the director said when Nicholas asked him what he thought?

_____

_____

_____

I can perfectly understand if you wrote that he said he did not like it, or at least several aspects of it. That was certainly what Nicholas thought at the end of many weeks of work to produce the programme. He felt rather depressed.

What the director actually **said** was:

'That was very good indeed – it does pretty well everything I want it to and we shouldn't need to make any substantial changes. Thank you very much.'

This true story shows that even non-verbal communication isn't wholly straightforward.

The personnel manager explained afterwards that her boss had a nervous tic, an involuntary shake of the head every minute or so – 18 times during the programme. She knew him and so was unconcerned by his mannerism – but perhaps it would have been helpful if she had mentioned it beforehand to Nicholas!

No deception was intended in this example, but I expect you have met the person who wears a cheery smile when greeting you, shakes your hand warmly, then tells you that you have failed an exam, been passed over for promotion or delegated a particularly obnoxious task.

Here, the communicator is trying to convey a feeling of **good news** via the body language while giving you **bad news** verbally. The hope is that you will receive the powerful non-verbal message more clearly than the verbal one which you are not likely to enjoy hearing.

Often, the speaker will then hurry off, before you have had time to resolve the conflicting messages sent.

2.5 Knowing your people

Nicholas couldn't get to know the director who was sending the conflicting signals. That will be the case for many people you meet in the ordinary course of events, like occasional customers.

But it shouldn't be true of your own team, or of other people that you meet regularly, such as colleagues from other departments, regular customers and suppliers.

Observe your regular contacts, and find out their individual traits. This will help you to adjust your approach to them in line with the signals you are receiving.

2.6 Tone of voice – the sound equivalent of body language

Studies of verbal communication have shown that **how** you say something can have more effect on your listener than **what** you say. It has been observed that people respond far more to the **tone** in which something is said than to its actual content. If your tone of voice conflicts with the message delivered, the listener will respond to the tone rather than the words.

'Don't look at me in that tone of voice!'

This is a jocular remark which conveys a number of points about verbal and non-verbal communication.

The **tone of voice** you use conveys far more to your listener than your actual **words**. It is the equivalent of body language, and very important.

Activity 29 · 2 mins

Look at the following four messages which you might need to deliver to your team. Then choose **one** appropriate tone of voice in which to deliver them from the following list.

Tones to use: persuasive; sombre; upbeat; sad; encouraging; persistent; buoyant; angry; hectoring; downbeat; congratulatory; dismal; welcoming; cheerful; convincing; humble.

The message	The appropriate tone
1 Announcing that a former colleague has died after a long illness.	
2 Seeking sponsorship for a fund raising event which your organization is helping to organize for a local charity.	
3 Reviewing the third set of progressively worse monthly performance figures for your department, two weeks after a new competitor opened premises nearby.	
4 Informing your team that the independent quality audit carried out recently has given your department a percentage score in the upper 90s for compliance with standards.	

My suggested answer is provided on page 93.

You may have chosen tones other than those indicated there, because of differences in how you perceive the meanings of words. One person may choose 'sombre' when another would use 'sad.'

Nevertheless, there are a number of words which would have been inappropriate to any of the messages and would have created an instant barrier between speaker and audience. I'm thinking of: hectoring; dismal; persistent; angry; humble.

As soon as you begin to speak, your audience – whether one person or a hundred – will grasp your tone of voice and respond to it, even before they hear the words you are using. And if they respond badly to the tone, they may hardly hear the words at all. For example:

- if you deliver the bad news about performance in an angry or hectoring tone, the chances are that people will become defensive or resentful and look to divert any blame from themselves – after all, aren't you their leader?
- if you seek support for a charity in a persistent tone, they may respond by thinking of every charity they already support and asking themselves why they should do any more;
- humility has been so overworked by politicians and public figures generally that it almost inevitably sounds insincere;
- a dismal tone may simply depress and detract from (say) the merits and achievements of the person who has died, or it may discourage your team from trying to achieve better performance in a difficult working situation. 'What's the point of trying?' is the message they may receive from a depressing tone of voice.

Swearing, flippancy, sarcasm and jokes

Beware of these.

Even if the team **swear** among themselves, they may not appreciate it coming from their first line manager – they may find it insulting and patronizing.

Telling **jokes**, or adopting a **flippant** or **sarcastic** tone, can often cause offence and detract from the message being conveyed.

As a general rule, it is wise to steer clear of all such behaviour.

Of course, there can be exceptions to this rule. Occasional touches of humour to lighten the day are well advised, but jokes are best left to professional comedians since many jokes are described as being in bad taste – a reference to another of our senses.

'Laddish' behaviour, including foul language, sexual innuendo and racist remarks are increasingly cited in Employment Tribunals reviewing cases of constructive dismissal, i.e. where an employee feels that he or she has been driven out of their job by the obnoxious conduct of working colleagues.

Activity 30 · ⏱ 3 mins

Can you think of an example, from your own experience, of a situation in which it is appropriate to use a tone of voice which conflicts with the message which you are delivering? Describe it briefly.

_____

_____

_____

Your answer will depend entirely on your own background and situation. Here are a couple of general examples, both to do with maintaining the morale of any team.

■ You know, as the first line manager, that the situation is grave and can be saved only by extreme effort. You would then be correct to present the facts as they are, but to do so in a defiant, upbeat way. This can imply to your team that there is hope, provided that they are prepared to make the effort required. To sound dismal and defeatist could make the possible calamity into a certainty.

■ If the results are good, but you know they are due more to good fortune than good work (perhaps a competitor was closed for some reason), then you may deliver the good news in a relatively downbeat way, while sticking to the facts as they are. This can prevent the team members from feeling too pleased with themselves, and inspire them to make the next results even better through their own efforts.

3 Sending, receiving and interpreting unspoken messages

Non-verbal communication is a powerful tool – and as a first line manager you want to use it in a positive way.

3.1 Setting an example with behaviour

To a certain extent team members take their cue from their manager.

Activity 31

3 mins

Here are three scenarios. Read them through and circle what you think of the example being set by the team leader.

Scenario	Is the Example . . .
1 Magnolia briefed her staff of ten people on wearing shop uniforms at all times as specified, 'even when the weather was hot'. The following week was very hot and she rebuked one staff member for appearing without her hat. Later that day, when she was cashing up after the shop was closed, she was seen by the same member of staff with her hat off and overall undone.	Poor Indifferent Good
2 At a briefing Jonathan stressed to his team the importance of being smart at all times while on duty, and keeping company vehicles 'as smart as you would want your own to be'. The next day, he took a new employee, Ben, to see a customer in his van which was dirty inside and out.	Poor Indifferent Good
3 Gemma was known to be strict about dress and housekeeping in her section, always smart and willing to act herself to clear up stray items of packaging, spillages and general litter. She demanded that her staff do the same. The section had the lowest accident rate on the site.	Poor Indifferent Good

Well I thought that the managers were 'indifferent' or 'poor' in scenario 1, 'poor' in scenario 2 and 'good' in scenario 3. Only Gemma was setting a consistently good example; Jonathan was probably setting a consistently bad one.

Gemma's team was following her good example – and there is a good chance that Ben, as a new employee, will follow Jonathan's.

Setting a **good** personal example is one of the most powerful non-verbal signals you can send to your team and more widely through your organization:

'**Watch me and do as I do**'

whereas the approach of:

'**Don't do as I do, do as I tell you**'

will fail sooner rather than later.

> In every aspect of life, actions speak louder than words.

3.2 Personal appearance

Two of the examples in Activity 31 refer indirectly to personal appearance, something which sends signals to everyone we meet.

Maybe your team has to conform to certain standards at work which are contentious in an age which favours 'dressing down'. Even here, there is a great deal of difference between being casual and being scruffy, half asleep or downright unhygienic.

> Some police forces are considering a switch back to older-style uniforms. They have found that the newer paramilitary look is intimidating and discourages members of the public from approaching them.

Many organizations require employees to wear uniforms or to conform to set standards of dress in other ways. These will vary according to the job being done and the working environment. What is suitable for someone working in a casino will differ greatly from an employee working in a catering kitchen, a foundry or as a security guard.

Whatever the dress or standard, how it is worn and the general appearance of the wearer sends strong signals to fellow employees, customers and the general public long before they have actually spoken to the person.

The uniform design itself can give off signals. On occasions you have to wonder whether they are the right signals.

Activity 32

3 mins

Both these employees begin work at around 4 am each day. Employee 1, Neil, is a delivery driver for a food distribution firm. Employee 2, Peter, is a postman. They work similar unsociable hours, and both meet both customers and members of the general public as a regular aspect of their job.

Appearance factor	Neil	Peter
Vehicle (exterior)	Clean, washed frequently at base	Clean, washed frequently per standing orders
Vehicle (interior)	Untidy	Clean and tidy
Uniform	Overall, scruffy and stained, carries company logo	Smart shirt, tie and trousers
Shoes	Trainers	Safety footwear, unpolished
Hair	Unkempt	Long, but tied back neatly
Facial appearance	Unshaven, bleary-eyed, teeth in need of attention	Clean-shaven, alert, teeth well cared for
Breath	Questionable	OK
Hands and nails	Vaguely clean, dirty fingernails	Clean and with clean nails

Taking 100% as ideal, how would you rate the messages that Neil and Peter communicate through their personal appearance?

_____

_____

I rated Peter very highly – around 90% based on the factors described. I gave Neil nearer 10%.

Peter is giving a very good general impression of himself and (via his uniform) his organization to everyone he meets, even if he never says anything at all to them.

Neil, who carries his company logo on his overall, is giving quite the opposite impression. He may be a diligent, helpful employee in the way he does his job, but the non-verbal communication which he sends will probably make people highly dubious about the performance standards of a man who is, after all, involved with food distribution. People react differently to the personal appearance of others and the signals which they respond to from associated matters affecting the senses of **scent** and **touch**. The circumstances in which people work also affect what it is reasonable to expect. For example:

- it is unreasonable to expect a mechanic who works in an exhaust centre to have immaculately clean hands at all times;
- someone who works in a smoky atmosphere, like a public house or betting shop, will inevitably have some cigarette smoke odours clinging to them.

Allowing for such occupational factors, there is a whole range of body language which either offends or encourages most people.

Activity 33

Make a list of the non-verbal factors associated with appearance, scent or touch (for example, nature of handshake):

- which 'turn you off' when meeting other people;
- which encourage you, before anything is actually said.

List as many factors as you can within the time suggested.

Sense	Body language which turns you off	Body language which encourages you
Sight		
Scent		
Touch		

EXTENSION 3
provides a list of body
language factors which
offend or please people
in workplace situations.

Like me, you probably listed more factors under 'Sight' (appearance) than the others, as we take in so much information through our eyes. However, an offensive (to the receiver) odour or over-familiar physical greeting may give much more immediate offence than a day's growth of beard or a creased uniform.

Nevertheless, it is possible to list a range of likes and dislikes that are shared by many people. Such a list is given as Extension 3.

3.3 Managing non-verbal communication

Though taste has not been included in the list there are ways of sending positive signals using this sense. Providing good food as an act of hospitality is a way of saying an unspoken welcome to guests, personal or paying.

Intrinsic factors

Throughout this session, we have concentrated on the aspects of non-verbal communication which can be controlled by their sender and influenced by their manager.

The sender of a message cannot control sheer prejudice by the receiver against someone because of the colour of their hair, skin or eyes, their sex or a disability. Such prejudices, if they are translated into discriminatory employment practices, are illegal in the UK.

Controllable factors . . .

However, people of any race may behave in a way which sends the wrong signals to people who are **not** prejudiced, including those of their own race. Many such signals appear in Extension 3. These aspects of behaviour can be **managed** by the individuals and **influenced** by their managers and team leaders towards the standard acceptable to the organization and its customers.

. . . in yourself and your team members

As first line manager, it is for you to set the standard for your team. Doing so tells them what you expect without the need for any potentially sensitive discussions. Once your team generally accepts the standard you set as their norm, that will exert pressure on any who are falling short of it. They will resent individuals letting the side down and back you directly or indirectly. Where individuals cannot or will not accept your standards and the established norm for their colleagues, then you will need to treat the matter as you would any other aspect of conduct falling short of the standards required, for example poor work performance, lateness for work, absentee-ism, and failure to observe safety rules to the letter.

The fact that you and the rest of the team achieve the organization's standard should make it much simpler for you to influence the person whose appearance and/or behaviour is out of line.

Mannerisms and nervous tics

There are sensitive issues involved in these matters. Just as no one can determine the colour of their eyes, nor can they always control nervous tics such as the one described in Activity 28.

Many idiosyncrasies should not offend anyone and some may find them attractive. Again, you need to distinguish between:

- what is just part of the person, such as rapid eye movements or a speech impediment; and
- what is controllable and may be a symptom of something else – boredom, aggression or nervousness – like looking at a watch frequently, pointing or wagging a finger, or a refusal to look a listener in the eye.

You will need to decide, in each case, whether the person concerned is sending unacceptable signals which it is in their power to control. Then you can decide what action, if any, you need to take.

Assertiveness and aggression

In some fields, notably the military and physical contact sports, a greater or lesser degree of **controlled** aggression is essential to achieve success.

Note carefully the word 'controlled'. Randomly aggressive conduct is not acceptable in any sphere – you must direct it at the 'enemy' or the 'other side'.

In most other walks of life, aggressiveness is discouraged but assertiveness is necessary and desirable, certainly in managers whose task is to achieve objectives through their teams – not to do the job for them.

So what is the difference between aggressive behaviour and assertive behaviour?

Activity 34

2 mins

Look at the following two situations and decide which is a case of aggressive behaviour and which is a case of assertive behaviour. Underline your choice in each case.

Driver 1, Bill, was approaching a roundabout in the inside lane of a busy dual carriageway, wishing to take the right-hand exit. The driver checked the mirror two hundred yards from the roundabout, saw a vehicle in the outside lane approaching rapidly about half a mile back, signalled to turn right and moved out smoothly into the outside lane.

Aggressive/Assertive

Driver 2, Ben, was approaching a roundabout in the outside lane of a dual carriageway saw a queue of vehicles in the outside lane, all evidently wishing to turn right. The driver moved back into the inside lane, drove inside the line of waiting vehicles to the roundabout entrance, then indicated to turn right and accelerated rapidly to reach the circle before the leading vehicle in the queue.

Aggressive/Assertive

I used a motoring example as most readers will surely have experienced aggressive behaviour from other motorists. I would certainly label the first behaviour assertive and the second aggressive.

The difference between them is that:

- assertive behaviour on Bill's part respects the rights of other people, but makes sure that his objectives are achieved;
- aggressive behaviour on Ben's part fails to respect the rights of others or simply doesn't accept that they have any. It is likely to provoke an equal and opposite reaction from the person it is imposed upon.

In most working situations:

- **aggressive behaviour** is undesirable and may lead to serious disciplinary problems;
- **assertive behaviour** is desirable and essential in first line managers and team leaders;
- **weak behaviour** is undesirable and will lead to a failure to meet objectives and satisfy customers, fellow employees and, ultimately, anyone – including the person exhibiting it.

All three kinds of behaviour show up clearly in body language and non-verbal communication.

Activity 35

5 mins

Try to classify each of the following behaviours as assertive, aggressive or weak.

Behaviour	Weak	Assertive	Aggressive
1 Jabbing finger at someone when giving an instruction			
2 Maintaining frequent eye contact during counselling interview			
3 Fiddling with papers and looking down when disciplining employee			
4 Leaning forward and smiling at applicant during a selection interview			
5 Standing over a trainee during an 'on job' training session			
6 Turning away from employee when announcing bad news about a job application			

You probably decided that 1 and 5 were examples of aggressive behaviour; 2 and 4 displayed assertive behaviour; 3 and 6 suggested weak behaviour.

So far as you are able, you need to set a positive, assertive example to your team and all the other people with whom you have dealings through the body language which you exhibit.

A checklist is provided for you as Extension 4 as a reasonable norm of assertive behaviour in business. You should use it to compare with both your own style and with that of members of your team as they behave towards you and their peers.

You can then decide if you need to do anything in terms of self improvement, counselling or more formal training for yourself or members of your team.

4 Attitude, perceptions and cultures

EXTENSION 4
is a checklist for
assertive behaviour in
the workplace.

Many personal, subjective factors are involved in the reactions of people to body language. There are cultural factors too. For example:

- films have been made showing how far Japanese people will go to avoid touching each other, even in the most crowded situations – they become very apparent viewed in slow motion;
- many races are much more demonstrative physically when they meet than are, for example, English people (as a general norm);
- in many countries, people shake hands with everybody in the office before beginning work, which again is not the norm in the UK.

If you work with people from different cultural backgrounds, or work abroad yourself sometimes, you need to be aware of differences that affect how non-verbal communications are interpreted.

One factory surveyed in the south of England revealed more than 20 languages in use other than English. Many of these languages will be associated with cultures which may traditionally view body language differently from each other and from the norm for the UK.

Because of the mix in many workplaces, there can be no hard and fast rules that will work for every situation. But if you get to know your team as individuals, you will discover which aspects of body language in your workplace may be interpreted differently by people from other backgrounds.

The mix in every team is different. If you move from a team where one set of perceptions exists to one where another quite different set has developed, you may need to adjust your own approach to take account of the different environment.

Activity 36 · 30 mins

S/NVQ D1.2

List as many examples of non-verbal communication used in your own organization for the five senses as you can. Here are some ideas:

■ sight – including safety or advertising posters and performance graphs;

■ sound – **excluding** speech, but including audible signals like vehicle-reversing warnings;

■ touch – perhaps used in noisy environments;

■ smell – warning smells introduced into hazardous chemicals, or appetising aromas (like roasting coffee) channelled onto pavements to communicate with customers;

■ taste – such as samples given to potential customers, or to check the quality of products.

_____

_____

_____

_____

_____

_____

When you have finalized your list, try to think of further uses for powerful non-verbal communication channels which could be used for any purpose. Prepare recommendations accordingly to discuss with your team and your manager.

_____

_____

_____

_____

_____

_____

Self-assessment 3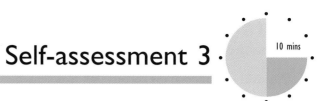

10 mins

1   The five senses with which we can receive information are hearing,

_____, _____, _____, and _____.

2   Which conveys most information to your listener: the words which you say,
or the tone of voice which you use?

_____

3   You need to _____ your team members as individuals in order to

_____ the non-verbal communication which you _____

from them.

4   The difference between assertive behaviour and aggressive behaviour is
that

_____

5   Name two things which you should beware of when speaking to your team,
individually or as a group.

_____

6   Give an example of a situation where it is legitimate for your body language
to contradict the verbal message which you are giving.

_____

The answers to these questions can be found on page 89.

5 Summary

- We take in information through all five senses.

- Too much emphasis is often placed on the spoken and written word which are relatively new channels of communication.

- Non-verbal communication or body language accounts for more than half of the information which we absorb.

- In spoken communication, the **tone** which you use is many times more important than the **words** which you use. Using the wrong tone can prevent people hearing your words at all.

- **Unconscious** non-verbal communication is swift, powerful and very good at telling us about emotional states like fear, anger, despair and joy.

- **Conscious** spoken or written language can convey more subtle shades of meaning but takes longer to organize, transmit and interpret.

- You need to know your people and their typical body language – and how they will respond to yours.

- Setting a good example in dress, approach to work and the language and tone of voice which you use is the best non-verbal communication you can transmit.

- Team leaders must learn to manage their own body language and be ready to influence their team to meet the organization's standards.

- Assertive behaviour is the normal pattern required of a first line manager. Both aggressive and weak behaviour will lead to problems between the manager and the team and within the team itself.

Performance checks

1 Quick quiz

Question 1   What is the rough maximum number of people with whom it is practicable to communicate as a team?

_____

Question 2   When you receive a communication, what are the three decisions you could take as to what to do with it?

_____

_____

_____

Question 3   If you are using codes, or abbreviations such as those found in text messaging, what must you and the receiver share?

_____

Question 4   What is the aim of normal management communication?

_____

Question 5   What do you consider a reasonable length of time for a team briefing? How frequently should they be held? Circle your preferred answer.

- 5/10 minutes every week
- 15/20 minutes every fortnight
- 45/60 minutes once per month.

Question 6   Complete the following sentence:

Briefing individuals is ineffective and inefficient because

_____

_____

Question 7   What is the first question you should ask yourself before sending any communication?

_____

Question 8   Provide any two of the eight key questions to ask when choosing the most effective communication channel for any purpose?

_____

_____

_____

_____

Question 9   'It is important to tell people **why** you need them to do something.'

Do you agree or disagree with that statement? Explain your reasons in one sentence.

_____

Question 10   How can a listener improve his or her concentration?

_____

Question 11   Give two examples each of:

- assertive body language
- weak body language
- aggressive body language

Question 12   Complete the following sentence:

'Don't do as I do, do as I tell you' is a very ineffective way of managing a team because

_____

_____

Answers to these questions will be found on pages 93–94.

2 Workbook assessment

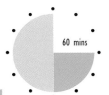

60 mins

Please read through the following case study and then tackle the assignment which follows it, writing your suggestions on a separate sheet of paper.

Terry Newbury had just moved from a department in which she had successfully served for some years, first as an operator and then as a section leader. Now she had the chance to become a first line manager – but she was warned that it would be no 'bed of roses', as morale in her new department was low. The 12 people in it feared their jobs were on the line, as their work could be contracted out to a larger specialist plant a few miles away. Terry's new boss assured her that this wasn't intended to happen, but that unless their performance improved – and they stopped taking time off for no good reason – they might bring about the very result that they feared. A £250,000 investment programme had been put on ice but it could be re-instated swiftly if standards improved.

Terry's predecessor, Harry Mallow, had been known as a strict disciplinarian, with a straight back, jutting chin, fierce gaze and military bearing. He was an expert on the complex plant used, having helped install the machines many years before most of the employees had arrived. He had conducted regular monthly briefings, usually backed by complex technical slides about the machines and slides of detailed performance figures for the past month. Though he finished every session by saying 'Any questions now?', few were ever asked. Harry was always able to fix problems with the machines, in a way which Terry knew she would not be capable of for a long time, if ever. Harry always brought sandwiches for his meal break and never mingled with the operators except on a strictly business basis.

When Terry met the team, she found that most of them had gloomy expressions and assumed that she had been put in to close the department down.

'After all' said one of the older hands 'You know nothing at all about the job, so what else can you do? 'Cept sitting in your office reading the bad news old "Happy Harry" used to be so pleased to "share with us", as he called it after the communication course they sent him on.'

Another said 'Don't tell us again about that quarter of a million they tell us they might spend here – the word on the grapevine is it's only to keep us going till they're ready to close us down. They treat us like donkeys anyway – so which are you, the one with the carrot or the one with the stick?'

If you were in Terry's situation, what could you do to:

■ address the barriers to communication you see;
■ send positive non-verbal messages to her new team;
■ choose the most appropriate means of communicating her messages to them;
■ gain their trust in and commitment to the proposed investment scheme.

Draw on your own experience, and on the work you've done throughout this workbook, to provide a skeleton for your plan. You can assume that the investment is a genuine possibility.

3 Work-based assignment

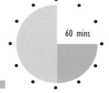

60 mins

S/NVQ D1.2

The time guide for this assignment gives you an approximate idea of how long it is likely to take you to write up your findings. You will find you need to spend some additional time gathering information, talking to colleagues and thinking about the assignment. The result of your efforts should be presented on separate sheets of paper.

Your written response to this assignment may form useful evidence for your S/NVQ portfolio. The assignment is designed to help you demonstrate your personal competence in:

■ communicating;
■ influencing others.

First, look at the methods/channels through which you are asked to provide information within your department or to other parts of the organization.

Next, take one major method/channel and try to follow through thoroughly what happens to the information.

- Is it used?
- Is it filed – and if so for what purpose?
- Does it cause anything to happen?
- What non-verbal reactions do you observe in people who you ask about the usefulness of what you send them?

Then summarize your conclusions and make recommendations as to whether the organization should:

- scrap the information;
- continue as now;
- make improvements.

Remember your aim should be to make all communication:

- effective – doing the right thing;
- efficient – working as well as possible at optimum cost.
  Now discuss your conclusions and recommendations with all the people involved with that specific communication cycle. Try to convince them of any changes you wish to see, through:

- clear presentation of the facts;
- appropriate use of assertiveness in putting your case across.

Reflect and review

1 Reflect and review

Now that you have completed this workbook, you can review what you have learned against the objectives set for it. Our first objective was to:

■ **understand how important it is that there is clear communication throughout the working environment**

Good management is impossible without effective communication, as management is the art of achieving results through people. If people aren't given the information they need, then how can they be expected to understand and do what is required of them?

■ List some essential ways in which communication can be improved in your own area of activity:

(1) between you and members of your team

_____

_____

_____

_____

(2) between you and your immediate manager

_____

_____

_____

_____

(3) between you and people in other departments you need to communicate with.

_____

_____

_____

_____

Your next objective was to:

■ **recognize and overcome barriers to communication**

The responsibility for communicating rests clearly with the sender of information. Most of the barriers are erected by the sender. Many of them have been referred to and illustrated in the text.

■ Note some barriers which you are now more aware of and the actions which you can take, or influence others to take, to remove or reduce them.

_____

_____

_____

_____

We have seen that an important way of preventing barriers from arising is to send the message using a appropriate channel of communication, so our next objective was to:

■ **select and use the method of communication which is most suited to the circumstances**

There is no perfect communication solution which will work in every situation and it is vital to choose the best channel, or combination of channels, for each individual need.

■ Look at the various channels used in your area and decide whether they are effective currently, or need change or reinforcement to improve their effectiveness.

_____

_____

_____

_____

Having sent our message, we saw next how important it is to ensure that it has been both received and understood, so meeting our next objective, to:

■ **check that messages are clearly received and understood, however they are sent**

Communication needs to flow in both directions between the sender and receiver of information. If feedback is not available, or is ignored, the quality and credibility of all information transmitted will deteriorate.

Make some recommendations to improve the quality of feedback which:

(1) you receive from your own team and others with whom you communicate on a regular basis

_____

_____

_____

_____

(2) you provide to your manager and other departments with whom you deal

_____

_____

_____

_____

More than half the information which people receive from you stems from the body language which they perceive, so our next objective was to:

■ **understand the power of non-verbal communication and to take it into account when you are both sending and receiving information**

If you get it wrong frequently, it will form a major barrier to communication with your team and they may never hear your spoken messages clearly or at all.

■ Are there some ways in which you can improve your communication effectiveness in this area, using both the checklist provided in Extension 4 and the materials from Session C generally to help you?

You might like to enlist the help of a trusted friend and colleague, from work or private life, to obtain a friendly second opinion.

_____

_____

_____

_____

Our final workbook objective was to:

■ **recognize and respond to body language and behaviour**

You need to interpret accurately the signals which you receive from other people, especially those coming from your own team, and from immediate contacts in your working life.

■ List up to three aspects of the behaviour you see which should be addressed, or learned from, to provide an example for you and members of your team.

_____

_____

_____

2 Action Plan

Use this plan to develop for yourself the course of action you want to take. Note in the left-hand column the issues or problems you wish to tackle; then decide what you intend to do and make a note in column 2.

The resources you need might include time, money, information or materials. You may need to negotiate for some of them, but they could be something that is easily acquired, like half an hour of somebody's time, or a chapter of a book. Put whatever you need in column 3. No plan means anything without a timescale, so put a realistic target completion date in column 4.

Finally, describe the outcome you want to achieve as a result of this plan, whether it is for your own benefit or advancement, or a more efficient way of doing things

Desired outcomes			
1 Issues	2 Action	3 Resources	4 Target completion
Actual outcomes			

3 Extensions

Extension 1   Phonetic alphabet

A = Alpha	J = Julia	S = Sierra
B = Bravo	K = Kilo	T = Tango
C = Charlie	L = Lima	U = Uniform
D = Delta	M = Mike	V = Victor
E = Echo	N = November	W = Whiskey
F = Foxtrot	O = Oscar	X = X Ray
G = Golf	P = Papa	Y = Yankee
H = Hotel	Q = Quebec	Z = Zulu
I = India	R = Romeo	

Extension 2

Book	*Body Language at Work*
Author	Adrian Furnham
Edition	1999
Publisher	CIPD

Extension 3

The following aspects of body language which people frequently find unpleasant or encouraging may well appear in your lists, but they are **not** intended to be comprehensive, and you may have listed other items. However, this list, based on the opinions of large numbers of interviewees, is likely to include many items in common with yours.

Sense	Body language and associated matters which turn people off	Body language which encourages people to GO to the next stage
Sight	■ Untidy clothes ■ Inappropriate dress for situation, e.g. beachwear or shorts in the office ■ Stubble ■ Untidy/unwashed hair ■ Inappropriate makeup ■ Badly worn/untidy uniforms ■ Quirky dress at odds with workplace situation ■ Scowling/seemingly hostile manner ■ Bored manner/yawning ■ Attending to other people, e.g. colleagues, computer screens; radios or TV screens ■ Eating, drinking – or the remains of meals left on view ■ Smoking/dirty ashtrays ■ Slovenly posture/leaning on the counter ■ Turning back on listener ■ Hung-over appearance – head down, shoulders slumped	■ Smart, business like appearance ■ Friendly smile ■ Make-up appropriate to the workplace situation ■ Clean shaven appearance or trimmed beard/moustache, etc. ■ Tidy/clean hair ■ Welcoming attitude ■ Alert, ready-for-business manner ■ Giving undivided attention ■ Looking at you while speaking
Scent	■ Over-strong perfume or after-shave ■ Cigarette smoke ■ Alcohol on breath ■ Strong foodstuffs on breath – garlic, onions ■ Generally unpleasant odour ■ Inappropriate perfume ■ Bad breath	■ Discreet perfume ■ Neutral scent ■ Sweet breath
Touch	■ Flabby handshake ■ Over-firm handshake ■ Touching in any way e.g. clapping on the back; patting shoulder, overlong handshake ■ Standing over one, invading one's personal space	■ Firm, friendly handshake ■ Respecting customs and cultural norms, e.g. not touching ■ Sympathetic touch in appropriate circumstance ■ Respecting personal space

Extension 4

Checklist for assertive behaviour		
Aspect	**Comment**	**How do I compare?**
1 Maintain frequent eye contact with your listeners	Both holds their attention and gives you instant feedback on the effectiveness of your communication	
2 Use a range of facial expressions to support your message	A fixed stare conveys aggression. Using a range of expressions suited to the message will help reinforce your message	
3 Maintain an upright, relaxed posture	Whether you are standing or sitting, this will convey alertness and interest in your listeners	
4 Use open, confident gestures	A firm handshake and open gestures with the palms outwards convey sincerity and openness. Folding arms across the chest implies defensiveness and withdrawal	
5 Set a good example at all times	This will assert that you are practising what you preach and will make it hard for your team to go against your requests and instructions	

4 Answers to self-assessment questions

Self-assessment 1 on page 20

1 GIGO stands for 'garbage in, garbage out'. It warns us that no matter how sophisticated the means of communication used, it will not improve the quality of an ill-prepared or wrong message.

2 No manager, however able, can communicate effectively with a team of more than 12 or so people. Above that number, it becomes impossible to know them and takes too long simply to deal with the inevitable day-to-day problems which arise.

3 The communication cycle describes the communication process in terms of inputs, processing and outputs, plus feedback.

4 The main stages in communication are:
receiving; decoding; processing; encoding and transmitting/sending

5 All managers must be skilled **COMMUNICATORS** because their job is about **GETTING THINGS** done through **OTHER** people who must be informed what is **REQUIRED** of them.

6 Five barriers to verbal communication could include:

- language;
- accent/tone of voice;
- speed of delivery;
- jargon/blinding with science;
- lack of a clear message.

7 A practical limit to the size of a group to be briefed would be 12. This is a generally recognized upper limit.

8 Six features of an effective team briefing are:

- grasp of the subject by the speaker;
- preparation;
- clear messages/delivery;
- venue free of noise and distraction;
- suitable timing;
- checking understanding.

9 The grapevine is an informal communication network, which provides information that management will not give, or only provides in an ineffective way.

10 **GIVING INDIVIDUAL FEEDBACK** and **PROVIDING INFORMATION** are examples of situations where **ONE** to **ONE** communication is appropriate.

11 Examples of barriers to effective written communication are:

- illegible handwriting;
- bad spelling/misuse of words;
- poor grammar, distorting the meaning;
- excessive length leading to information overload;
- unfamiliar acronyms and abbreviations;
- tiny print – as in credit agreements and insurance policies.

Self-assessment 2 on page 48

1 The best option to use for any communication is the one which combines **EFFECTIVENESS** with **EFFICIENCY**.

2 The **PHONETIC** alphabet is an **INTERNATIONALLY** recognized system for **ENSURING** that oral messages are received **ACCURATELY**.

3 (7) How simple is it to use?
  (8) How quickly can it be done?

4 Information overload is the situation where so much information arrives that the receiver is unable to absorb it and decide which part of it is actually relevant and requires action.

5 Tell them what you are going to tell them. Tell them. Tell them what you've told them.

6 How, What/Which, Where, When, Who/To Whom, Why.

  Generally open questions encourage people to open up and give you more information. They are very useful for obtaining feedback.

7 Communication needs to be two-way, so that both parties are involved in both giving and receiving information. If the flow of information is all in one direction, then the quality of the message will become progressively less effective.

8 (1) 'Is there anything else we need to cover for now?' – **controlling** the interview.
  (2) 'Have I dealt with the points you made in your question?' – **confirming** something with the other party to the communication.

9 (1) In an emergency, where there is no time to discuss a course of action which needs to be taken immediately.

(2) In a routine matter, where both parties are following a sequence of events in which they are both well versed, such as a procedure in an operating theatre or a physical training drill.

Self-assessment 3 on page 71

1 The five senses with which we can receive information are hearing, **SIGHT, TOUCH, SMELL** and **TASTE**.

2 The tone of voice is far more communicative – get it wrong and your listeners will hardly listen to the words at all.

3 You need to **KNOW** your team members as individuals in order to **INTERPRET/UNDERSTAND** the non-verbal communication which you **RECEIVE** from them.

4 The difference between assertive behaviour and aggressive behaviour is that assertive behaviour respects the rights of other people, but aggressive behaviour ignores or tramples upon them.

5 Any two chosen from: swearing, flippancy, sarcasm, jokes.

6 This would be justifiable when, for example, you need to inspire your team to overcome immediate or longer term difficulties. The facts you have to give them may be unpalatable, but your body language must be positive and confident. If you are downbeat then they will think that you see no way out – so why should they try?

5 Answers to activities

Activity 12
on page 19

The message which the general actually sent was:

'Send reinforcements, we're going to advance.'

If you look at the sentence, it has the same number of syllables and rhythm as the distorted message that eventually arrived.

This, and many other stories like it, shows how hard it is to transmit a message **accurately** by word of mouth.

Activity 16
on page 29

	Option 1	Option 2	Option 3
Factors	**Notice on board**	**Email to everyone**	**Briefing for 20 people**
1	Most won't read	Many won't read	380 people not there but they may need to know
2	Very cheap	Relatively cheap	Quite expensive in time
3	Quick to do	Relatively quick	Needs time to arrange briefing
4	Official – no one can deny it is there	Semi-official, though we all know people don't read all their emails	The most affected will certainly know, but it still needs confirmation by official notice
5	Permanent – still there for new people to see	Impermanent – will be gone in hours or days. How will new people get to know ?	Impermanent – what about staff turnover?
6	No feedback	No feedback likely	Feedback chance from 20 people

Activity 17
on page 32

Channels used	Target Audience			
	Customers	**Employees**	**Suppliers**	**The media**
1 Face-to-face	X	X	X	X
2 Team briefings		X		
3 Notice boards		X		
4 Pagers		X		
5 Tannoy/public address	X	X		
6 Telephone (external/internal)	X	X	X	X
7 Fax	X		X	X
8 Emails	X	X	X	X
9 Internet	X		X	X
10 Intranet		X	X	
11 Overland post	X	X	X	X
12 Internal post		X		
13 Couriers	X		X	X
14 Mass meetings		X		
15 Corporate video	X	X	X	X
16 Advertising	X			
17 Group presentation, e.g. OHP, PowerPoint	X	X		X

Activity 18
on page 33

Channel	Communication Channels General Advantages and Aisadvantages					
	Certainty	**Permanence**	**Feedback available**	**Economy**	**Simplicity in use**	**Speed of use**
Oral	High	Low	High	Low	Low	High
Written	Medium	High	Low	Medium	Low	Low
Visual	High	Low	Medium	Low	Low	Low
Telephonic	Medium	Low	High	Low	High	High
Electronic	Low	Low	Medium	Medium	High	High

**Activity 19
on page 34**

THE SITUATION	RECOMMENDED CHANNEL
1 One of your delivery vehicles has had an accident and you need to advise customers that their deliveries will be affected.	Telephone seems the only choice. Because the need is so urgent and direct, certain contact with the customers is essential.
2 You are working on a new quality manual and your boss wants to eliminate as much paper as possible.	The intranet – if available – is a possibility. This would allow you to transmit the data to all approved users and they could simply print out information as and when needed. It would also be simpler to update than a large number of paper-based manuals.
3 You need to send a complicated draft mortgage offer to a client.	Post seems the surest and most economical channel. If there is urgency, a copy could be faxed initially, followed up by the postal copy.
4 You need to bring your team up-to-date concerning three serious near misses which have happened recently.	There seems no good option other than a face-to-face briefing for all the people concerned.
5 You need to check if seven people from other sites and departments can attend a sales meeting in three days' time.	Email could save a lot of phone calls. It puts all the facts before the receivers, so that they can check their commitments before replying – saving everyone time and phone costs.
6 Contractors' employees have been using the staff restaurant and cloakrooms without authorization.	Letter to their employer, reinforced by permanent notices on doors and verbal reminders from company staff will probably be the most effective solution – with the threat of exclusion from site to back it up.

**Activity 21
on page 39**

Taking each of the eight symptoms listed in turn, they should try to:

1 have an open mind and let the speaker convince them that the topic is interesting

2 focus on the content of what is being said – treating the style as nothing more than traffic noise or radio interference

3 count to ten – using any device to 'hold their peace' until sure that the speaker will not deal with the points of concern

4 ensure that fatigue is not self inflicted through late nights, etc.

5 keep the mind active and open to learning new things

6 look at the speaker and concentrate on what is being said – that will stop the mind wandering

7 be fair minded and give the speaker the same chance that they would ask for themselves

8 look for some area of interest in the subject other than their own.

Activity 29 on page 58

The suggested matches between messages and tones to use are:

1 sad or sombre

2 persuasive or convincing

3 sombre or downbeat

4 buoyant, congratulatory, cheerful or welcoming.

6 Answers to the quick quiz

Answer 1   Between ten and twelve members is the maximum desirable number.

Answer 2   1 No action required
2 Take action myself
3 Act through others – this should be your most frequent response.

Answer 3   Both the sender and the receiver of the message should have the same understanding of the code.

Answer 4   To send information to receivers, who need to do something as a result of being given the information.

Answer 5   Little and often is a good rule of thumb for briefings, so 5/10 minutes per week is much more likely to be effective than 45/60 minutes once a month.

Answer 6   Briefing individuals is ineffective and inefficient because it is likely that each individual will receive a slightly different message. In addition, the briefer will become bored and skimp on some aspects of the message.

Answer 7   Do I need to communicate this information at all? If the answer is 'no', then why am I doing it?

Answer 8   Do we need to communicate at all?
Will we reach all the people who need to know?
Can people deny having been told?
How long will it last?
Can we obtain feedback?
How much will it cost?
How simple is it to use?
How quickly can it be done?

Answer 9   It is important, because people are far more likely to co-operate if they understand the reasons for your request.

Answer 10   A listener can improve his or her concentration by looking directly at the speaker, which will both cut out distractions and give you an idea of the words being said from the shapes made by the speaker's mouth.

Answer 11   **Assertive** body language – maintaining eye contact; open gestures with the hands, friendly smile, firm handshake.
Weak body language – fiddling with papers or implements, shrinking away, refusal to look at speaker.
Aggressive body language – staring down; standing over; clenching or banging the fists; pointing or wagging fingers.

Answer 12   'Don't do as I do, do as I tell you' is a very ineffective way of managing a team because your team members will take in far more information from what you do than from what you say.

7 Certificate

Completion of this certificate by an authorized person shows that you have worked through all the parts of this workbook and satisfactorily completed the assessments. The certificate provides a record of what you have done that may be used for exemptions or as evidence of prior learning against other nationally certificated qualifications.

Pergamon Flexible Learning and ILM are always keen to refine and improve their products. One of the key sources of information to help this process are people who have just used the product. If you have any information or views, good or bad, please pass these on.